Heart Centered Revolutions Books

D1615651

Praise for Au . . . .

This small book packs a huge punch into the b.s. of so many teachings and "teachers" out today about being authentic. It's clear Bulbulia has lived what he writes about, including a number of personal experiences throughout his life that he's still learning from. This is the mark of humility. But his implores to stop listening to adopted, learned or assumed ways of being are incredibly powerful, if the reader can take in the words into the heart. This is the key point that to me is most compelling about this book, that anyone at all who's at all in touch with their own truth WILL find a familiar voice here. Including specific exercises or suggested games after each chapter is a necessary support for people who want to put into practice what the author encourages. I appreciate him doing that. I will be recommending this to my clients who are ready to take the next step out of their own set of lies and into their authenticity-led life.

- **Adam Gainsburg, Author and Founder of Soulsign.com**

There is immense power in being yourself, authentically. Adam shares this message through engaging accounts of his personal journey and professional experiences. Adam's ability to invite readers to accompany him via his experiences, and through his relatable language and practical exercises at the end of each chapter makes this not only a profound read but also a worthy book to return to time and time again; whenever a reminder is needed to follow our hearts and stay in our authentic selves even when the rest of the world may encourage otherwise. What a powerful reminder and practical tool to return us to our truest selves!

- **Judy Chan, Founder of AlliesinLife.com**

Adam has beautifully outlined a simple, yet powerful step-by-step process for individuals seeking the path to inner freedom through his book *Authenticity - The Immense Power to be Yourself*. Adam once again leads with conviction of his own beautiful heart, sharing his own personal journey with authenticity which enables the readers to deeply resonate with his profound wisdom. I highly recommend this book, and all of Adam's work, to those who are seeking to set themselves free from conformity and step more into their power and authenticity.

- **Veronica Paris, Intuitive Trauma Healer**

Thank you for giving me the opportunity to read an advance copy of this book. I'm not sure that I would've picked it up and read it without this little nudge. The fear of acknowledging that this is an area of my life that I needed to address had been preventing me from even touching a book on this subject. While it will most definitely be helpful in some deep issues in my life that

I'm not quite ready to address, it has been immediately helpful in the area of my life as a business owner. In my line of business, I can often get caught up in looking at what everyone else in the business is doing and thinking that I have to do the same in order to get the success that I think they have. Adam's book has helped me to return to the source of my authenticity. The place from where the vision for my business started and from where I sometimes stray from, my authentic self. This was a motivating reminder to stay true to myself so that I can have my own success by standing out from the rest instead of trying to be like everyone else.

- **Sandra Echavarria, Business Owner**

iv

Authenticity

THE IMMENSE POWER TO BE YOURSELF

Adam Bulbulia

HEART-CENTERED
REVOLUTIONS

FIRST EDITION

ISBN: 979-8-9860416-6-7

Terra Friedman King - Principal editor
Ann Marie Foley - Associate editor
William Moulton - Book and cover design

Foreword

I grew up in the Midwest. I learned "good" manners and to be polite. It's taken me ages to know what I truly feel under all my conditioning. Adam Bulbulia has helped me and so many others to express more of my own unique and unerring authenticity.

Adam's definition of authenticity is simply being yourself. He says, "It's a state of being completely real with what you're experiencing in the moment without hiding information, consciously filtering or modifying your natural state."

Do you sometimes feel it's not okay to feel the way you do? Do you believe there is an "appropriate" way of being? I know I've felt this way. I've found freedom in accessing my sometimes-messy authenticity and breathing life into moments by choosing to reveal what is really happening for me. Thankfully, it's a simple process to access our authenticity—we have only to feel what is in our heart for ourselves and for those we're with. Adam is here to help us do just that.

I know first-hand how gifted Adam is as a teacher. I met him as a Process Coaching trainer who taught classes I loved using perceptual tools and inner healing processes, as well as family constellation work. Adam is also a Board Certified Behavior Analyst, skillfully working with families of developmentally disabled and autistic youth and adults to support them in realizing their full potential. Working together at the nonprofit Heart-Centered Revolutions, I now know Adam as an inspired visionary. He'd truly love nothing more than to create a world that works for everyone by healing human disconnection with empathy and unconditional love. To do that, we're all being called to be our own radically authentic selves!

I'm excited for you to read this powerful book of short chapters with clarifying stories and potent exercises. You're about to begin a journey into (re)discovering your own innate authenticity. It's fun and easy to play with the perspective games that take core principles and make them immediately applicable in your life. Adam speaks truth in his "straight words," by showing us how to say what's on our heart. May you be inspired as your own organic authenticity emerges more fully!

~ *Ann Marie Foley*, life coach and director of operations at Heart-Centered Revolutions

After I had my daughter, I wanted to find a job that felt connected to my life purpose. I came across an ad for Bridging Worlds Behavioral Services which sparked something in my soul. When I met the owner, Adam Bulbulia, we had an interview unlike any other. Not only were we discussing how to be supportive to clients with autism and other disabilities, but how we can support ourselves through self-care and self-love. Tears of joy ran down my face. Within the first hour of meeting Adam, in a job interview no less, he helped me to feel myself on a profoundly deep level.

Through working with Adam, I've opened up to having more acceptance for where I am even when it's uncomfortable. One of the ways I've gained self-acceptance is through witnessing the way he is with our clients and families. Adam often says, "We want to practice having the same unconditional love and positive regard for ourselves as we do for the clients and families we serve." His message encourages all of us to have the courage to be our true, authentic selves.

At this point, I've been working with Adam for nearly a decade. A few years ago, I was honored to become the CEO. Adam has helped me see that the more vulnerable I am, the more I am able to embody the natural born leader within me.

I've had the opportunity to witness his creative process through the unfolding of this book. His dedication to embracing his authentic feelings throughout has been a fruitful journey of learning, growth, and healing. One of my favorite elements in this book are the games - I hope you have fun with them! They are so varied and unique. We have games to enhance your relationships, support you in the workplace, and guide you to connect more deeply with yourself. Similar to the way in which fire activates the seeds of a redwood tree, this book has helped spark my own authenticity. Authenticity is our sacred birthright.

~ *Samantha Cullity*, CEO
Bridging Worlds Behavioral Services

Preface

One day I awoke to find myself in a narcissistic and abusive cult. Tearing it to the ground and getting everyone else out is how I discovered my authenticity. This awakening freed my authentic voice and gave me a sense of truth I had never known before. After being in the group for 18 years, getting out was not easy.

It was 2020. After decades of vocational study, professional work, and deep psycho-spiritual development, something in my life was still tormenting me. So when the leader of the group suggested I try Iboga, I took a leap of faith. Iboga is an African psychedelic used in recovery from addiction and for psycho-spiritual development. *Bwiti* is the spiritual discipline associated with this medicine that several tribes in Gabon and Cameroon practice.

During the Iboga journey, I received a clear message from the medicine: I was following my mentor and not myself. The truth of this statement was very simple and profound. This truth turned my whole life inside out.

The medicine dropped me several layers deeper into my being. Things I used to be unsure about became crystal clear. After the journey, I knew what I wanted and what I didn't want. I could feel it in my body. As I reintegrated into daily life, this sense of authentic truth only grew deeper and stronger. I would no longer yield to suggestions from others when they felt wrong to me.

The more I spoke my truth, the more conflict brewed with the leader. Eventually, the leader of the cult read a piece of my writing expressing exactly what I felt about him, his psychological abuse, and his lack of integrity with the work he professed to embody. He accused me of being out of integrity and threw me out of the group, claiming it was for my own good. As he threw me out, he pressured me to donate my shares of our co-owned business back to the other partners. It was at that moment that I fully realized I was in a mind-controlling cult.

Over the next month and a half I did everything I could to communicate to everyone in the group about what I was seeing. At first, no one would listen. But the spark was alive, and after a crucial conversation this spark grew into a flame. Within about two months of my awakening to the cult, everyone was able to liberate themselves from the group except for the leader and his wife. For those of you who don't know what it's like to be in a cult, getting out is simply the first step in a long journey of recovering our authentic selves. At the time I got out, I didn't realize how long my true journey to recovery would be.

The process of liberating myself and supporting others in their liberation from the cult showed me many of my gifts in leadership. I came to realize that I was an extremely authentic person fiercely committed to honesty. I started to find my voice and truth in the world. I was no longer satisfied with following other leaders and wanted to collaborate with peers while being the biggest version of myself I could possibly be.

As I grew into this next layer of myself, I realized that not only was my fiancé acting in a toxically selfish way toward me, but so were the managers at my company, many of my staff, and about half of the people I had called my friends. I arrived at a crossroads. Should I continue to follow my mind and make life a comfortable place for manipulative people and thus deny myself? Or should I follow the truth of my heart even if it means some people will be uncomfortable with my authenticity and fall away from my life?

Samantha is my friend, musical partner, and a longtime employee at my company. Together, we improvised a song called "The Crossroads." Singing this song was a watershed moment. It was a point of no return, like crossing the Rubicon.[1] After singing this song, I knew the path I needed to walk to fulfill my destiny. While playing the guitar and singing, it became clear to me what I had to do with the company and what role Samantha was going to play. She sang herself into the leader position of the company as she helped guide me forward on my journey.

I drew a line in the sand and vowed to be completely honest and true to my heart moving forward–both at work and in my life. I let all the chips fall where they may. This led to lots of conflict as I entered into a complete revolution. Over the next five months, 20 of the 22 staff left or were fired as we reshaped the company in a way that was more congruent with our values. We wanted to create a company that works for everyone. To do that, I had to start with myself. I started prioritizing my truth over compromising and appeasing others to avoid conflict.

---

[1] It was when Julius Caesar crossed the Rubicon river against the Roman Senate's wishes that he put himself on course to become a leader and fulfill his destiny. Crossing this river was considered an act of war by the Roman Senate.

Authenticity became my new religion. I spoke the truth in every interaction and was no longer afraid to say anything to anyone at any time. When I initially came out of the closet as my authentic self, I was so full of repressed anger toward the cruelty and lies that were suddenly clear to me. I was furious at all the lies and manipulation in our culture. Anytime I sensed a micro-expression of hostility toward me or anyone else, I would fiercely state what I was perceiving. I did not realize how sensitive my awareness had become and how difficult some of my perceptions were for others to understand. I noticed how I was able to feel negative and unsafe energy somatically as a stab to my solar plexus. At the time, I was unaware how unique my perceptions were, and expected others to hear and accept my experience as valid truth.

I drank deeply from the well of inspiration. The stars shone brightly for me and I drew on the sun's rays each morning. I received a deep vision of a world that truly works for everyone. I began receiving profound visions of love, and was moved to do what I can to bring them into being. As a result, I founded Heart-Centered Revolutions, a nonprofit dedicated to making this a world that truly works for everyone. I became inspired to bring more empathy and unconditional love to this world. I completed my first two books and started 30 others on self-care, unconditional love, parenting, empathy, divisive energy, leadership, and so much more. My creativity that had been repressed for 18 years came bursting out.

The first edition of this book was called *Inspired Authenticity: The Power to Be Yourself in a World Full of Lies*. I was in the midst of dealing with all of the lies and narcissism that had been running my life and were still running our society. Fury raged in my newfound clarity.

Since then, I've been softening into a more expansive love for the world as it is. My heart still aches at the ills we face in the world. I'm continually learning to refine my authentic expression and attune it to wherever people are in their process. The first edition was fully authentic to my process at that time. The revised edition retains the strength of integrity from the first edition with softer elements and a deeper connection to a more universal truth. This revised edition is titled *Authenticity: The Immense Power to Be Yourself* because authenticity itself is an immense force of nature like the wind or thunder. Authenticity is an integral part of my life's mission and work. I believe it is part of each of our destiny paths. When we find our authentic way of being, it becomes crystal clear what we came here to do.

By turning our passion and energy toward what we love, the revolution of the heart is at hand. This is not a revolution of violence; it is a revolution of love within each of hearts. When any of us fully and truly become ourselves, the whole world blossoms. This is my vision for how authenticity can spread from person to person.

You are drawn to this book because you are a carrier of the seeds of authenticity. May these seeds be sown in your life, family, community, and work. May a truly authentic way of being take root and blossom in all our hearts and in our world.

Dedication

Most of what I've learned about authenticity has come from being with trees. Trees are remarkably authentic and honest. When I'm with trees, I get the distinct feeling that nothing is being hidden. The trees I've spent the most time with are part of an arboretum across the street from where I grew up in Short Hills, New Jersey–a small forest along the Connecticut River at Dartmouth College in Hanover, New Hampshire. Three Redwood Groves in California, one west of Ukiah and the other two are west of Occidental, have had a massive influence on me in the last 2 decades.

I dedicate this book to the preservation and restoration of the redwoods and all trees. The natives of this land called trees standing people. I, too, honor the sanctity of trees. Without them we would not be able to breathe and have life on this planet. None of us could be here without the trees. May we have trees for as long as our species exists and beyond. May the trees be treated with respect and dignity by humans now and for as long as we co-exist.

Similar to trees, the sun and the stars are remarkably authentic. They just are as they are and shine how they shine. They do not dim their light for anybody or have any hesitation about how they should be. I strive for my authenticity to be like the sunrise. May my words radiate off the page and touch your heart. May they light up your world of heart and soul the way the sun lights up the sky of our days.

I also admire the authenticity of Ralph Waldo Emerson, the most authentic writer I've ever encountered. His essay "Self-Reliance," and his writings about education are eternally written in my heart. If I can be as authentic as Ralph Waldo Emerson was in his writing, I will die a happy man. Along with Emerson, I want to thank Henry David Thoreau, William Wordsworth, Alanis Morissette, Terry Tempest Williams, William Blake, Walt Whitman, Carl Jung, Amanda Baggs, Martin Luther King Jr., Frederick Douglass, and Greta Thunberg. You have all taught me so much about how to be an authentic human being in the world. I wish I could meet you all in the flesh. I hope to meet and collaborate with those of you who are still living.

Samantha, you are so authentic and true. I don't know what I would do without you. Kari and Steve, you provide such a deep and profound authenticity to our leadership team at Bridging Worlds, thank you so much. Bill, Ann Marie, Theo, and Jayson your authenticity has all been exemplary in our work together at Heart-Centered Revolutions.

Most of all I dedicate this book to my dear father Ahmed Bulbulia. You were the most honest person I've ever known well. You were nothing but yourself every day that you lived. Thank you for being an upright and honest man in this world that doesn't always support authenticity. Thank you for embodying authenticity so fully and completely. With every word and every deed, I strive to be as authentic as you. My life is a living tribute to you, Dad. In every breath and every word you are here. Every time I learn to get a little more honest and take a stand for truth, I can hear the sound of your voice with a lilt of laughter as you gleefully said with your mixed British, South African, and American accent, "That's bullshit." I miss you so much—there is not a day that goes by that I don't wish you were here with me. Words cannot express the fullness of my love for you, Dad.

Acknowledgment

Thank you Terra Friedman King, who was our primary editor and helped to significantly refine this book. Thank you Ann Marie Foley for all the finish editing you did for this book. And thank you Bill Moulton for your artistic design and your production skills. The editing team was Terra, Ann Marie, and Adam. Bill is the artist who designed this cover and produced the book.

Revised Edition

This significantly revised edition of the book you are reading came after I went through a very angry phase of my life as I came out of the mind control cult I was in for 18 years. While my anger was completely authentic to my process at the time, some of the messages I wrote before the revision do not hold true to where I am today. It was a phase I needed to go through, but truly loving authenticity is much softer than I first realized. This book has been so significantly revised, including giving it a new sub-title, that we are considering this the first edition.

As I come into this softness, I have so many people to thank for helping me develop my authenticity. From my vantage point, some of these people have left the integrity of their beings. I call them "adversaries." An adversary is someone who takes a stand against the truth of your being. Adversaries are people who help test us and help us evolve.

If love is what we are after, then our intention for all adversaries is to return to a harmonious connection once they have come back to the authenticity of their being. This is what I believe Jesus meant when he told us to love our enemies.

In a sense, we recognize that love and connection exist underneath the apparent disconnection. My adversaries helped to inspire this book. They have helped me to develop more love in response to their resistance and refusal to accept the authenticity of my heart. My former mentor, teacher, and friend showed me how insecure I was and how to face that insecurity. My former fiancé showed me so much love and hatred, and taught me how to catch subtle, feeling nuances in a relationship. My former clinical director showed me how to see through fear and subterfuge in a way I never knew I could. My former best friend from college showed me what true friendship is and is not. My former martial arts instructor showed me how to take a stand for my values. And many of my former friends and acquaintances showed me how to not be held in a prison of excessively caring about what other people think of me. The more I stand on the ground of my values, the more deeply I can hold my truth even when others may not perceive it.

CONTENTS

SECTION II: Advanced Authenticity 88

Introduction

Authenticity is a state of being completely real with what one is experiencing in the moment without any need to hide information, consciously filter, or modify one's natural state. This rare state of being is greatly endangered on earth. Our society follows a set of laws, rules, and conditioning which promotes inauthenticity. Our society prioritizes "appropriate" behavior over sharing the truth of our hearts. For many of us, our true nature lives buried deep inside. It is often unwelcome and unable to come out.

Authenticity breathes life into existence. It helps us reveal the hidden treasures that are buried deep inside us all. As we begin to peer into the treasure trove of our individual authenticity, some essential questions may arise. How am I supposed to be? How am I supposed to live? What is the right decision for me to make? These questions have plagued humans for generations since we first fell away from our natural way of being. The Garden of Eden story from the Bible's Old Testament expresses this fall from innocence and connection. There are numerous tales in other traditions with a similar message. The human mind has separated us from our organic way of being. Don Miguel Ruiz calls this "the voice of knowledge."[2] Other traditions have referred to the mind as a parasite or predator that exists inside the human being, yet is not the human being. The Cree Indians called it Wendigo. Paul Levy called it wetiko in his book *Dispelling Wetiko*. We can stop this great fall from grace and loss of innocence. We can end the tale of the mind oppressing the heart inside ourselves now.

In this book I'm not going to tell you how to live and be yourself. I wouldn't profess to know that. Instead, I will share how I've stayed in touch with my essential self, how I've lost touch with my essential self, and how I've dedicated my life to allowing myself to be in my natural state. I've dedicated my life to embodying this kind of authenticity and supporting others to be in their natural state of authenticity as well. Perhaps some of the nuggets in this book will remind you of the truth inside your heart. My hope is that you can be the most authentic version of yourself possible.

---

[2] From Don Miguel Ruiz's book, *"The Voice of Knowledge: A Practical Guide to Inner Peace."*

The Essence of Authenticity

The reference guide below distills this entire book into five essential points, and will easily allow you to (re)familiarize yourself with the big takeaways. Of course I recommend you explore the entire book, complete with stories and games, to help you come more deeply into your own authentic way of being.

1. **Authenticity is Loving:** Authenticity is the most loving thing you can do for both yourself and others. When you are authentic, you tell others exactly what you need to say when you need to say it. You are true to yourself in the context of the situation.

2. **Meet Divisive Energy Honestly:** The biggest problem in humanity is getting taken over by what I call divisive energy. If you live without an understanding of divisive energy, you can get lost trying to love someone who is hurting you. Divisive energy is the energy that divides us. You can also call it selfishness or believing the ego, all of which point to the same thing. When we believe that we are separate and divided, we act from this place. Division then becomes our shared reality.

Meeting divisive energy with our hearts open allows us to discern honestly and set appropriate boundaries. Divisive energy can happen inside of us when we criticize ourselves for our organic way of being. It can also happen on the outside when someone judges us for being ourselves. When we meet divisive energy with honesty and an open heart, we find the best action to take to free ourselves from its grip. Serving love is the way through. Don't allow anyone to mistreat you—not even yourself.

3. **Authenticity is Liberating:** Being authentic will set you free. Once you start being authentic, you'll never want to go back to inauthenticity. You won't even mind some of the necessary conflicts that arise, once you experience how easy and effortless life can be when you are authentic. I call them "necessary" because the conflicts arise from simply being yourself. You do not seek them. They happen organically.

4. **Authenticity is the Key:** Living from your heart hinges on authenticity. What's un-conventional about the revolution of being truly yourself is that it doesn't come by

mobilizing in the streets, but from doing what you feel like doing naturally in your life. Authenticity is the key to the heart-centered revolution I've been dreaming of. Imagine how good life on earth could be when we create a world that works for everyone by healing human disconnection with empathy and unconditional love.

5. **Authenticity Works for the Good of All:** At times, it might seem as though the invitation to be true to yourself is another way to stop caring about others. That's not the full truth. Authenticity takes everyone into consideration, it's not just about being true to yourself. It's about being true to everyone else as well. When we are true to everyone, we honor the authenticity that is necessary to live in our world.

To be really true to yourself, you have to be true to everyone else. When you serve what is truly best for you, it also serves what's best for everyone else. And to truly serve the other, you must also work for your own good. This is the way our happiness and our beings are inextricably linked.[3] Embodying this principle creates a world that works for everyone.

Our egos create a world that works for no one. Left to their own devices, they would serve the self in a way that limits and blocks the flow of potential. I love my ego, but I'm not going to let it drive my actions. I'm also not going to let my actions be driven by other people's egos either. When we work for the good of their being over their ego, we are always working for their best interest. At heart, all loving beings want a world that works for the good of everyone.

---

[3] Related to the Martin Luther King Jr. quote: "In a real sense, all life is interrelated. All (Beings) are caught in an inescapable network of mutuality, tied in a single garment of destiny. Whatever affects one directly, affects all indirectly. I can never be what I ought to be until you are what you ought to be, and you can never be what you ought to be until I am what I ought to be... This is the interrelated structure of reality."

SECTION I: Authenticity, The Universal Basics

Authenticity comes in many shapes, sizes, and colors. I welcome your authentic and beautiful soul to blaze forth in whatever way you desire. I resolutely stand for authenticity. One of the reasons I love working with autistic and developmentally disabled people is that they often lack filters and are incredibly authentic. I feel so safe around authentic people.

This section is filled with stories in which I have embodied authenticity, been inspired by an expression of authenticity, or experienced what I consider to be inauthenticity. I find sharing stories of inauthenticity to be incredibly important because when we work with inauthenticity in its seed form, we can stop it from spreading much easier than when it becomes full blown.

I see the seeds of suicide in false apologies. I see the sprouts of homicide in words of blame. I see the currents of rape when our thoughts molest our feelings. I see the makings of genocide any time we condemn our own or another's inner experience.

Every act against the self is a microcosm of the widespread human violence in our world. All of the problems that exist on this planet are occurring within the human soul. Every time we betray ourselves in any way, great or small, we are acting from the self-destructive forces that are behind suicide. Anytime we attack someone with our words or deeds for simply being themselves, we are acting from the same forces that are involved in murder. Anytime we come against our feelings inwardly or another's feelings outwardly, we are engaged in the same forces that are behind all rape and sexual assault. Every time we judge our own or another's experience, we are engaged in the same forces that lead to discrimination, condemnation, and ultimately genocide. All genocide comes from condemning others simply for being themselves. When we can address these seed causes in our own heart, soul, and mind, we stand a true chance at changing the world to make it a more loving place.

We are the microcosm and the world is the macrocosm. Everything that exists in the human experience can be found inside each one of us. Just as a drop of seawater has the DNA of the whole ocean, so too are we inextricably intertwined with all of humanity. When we each take a stand for what is authentic in our own way with our hearts leading, only then will we be united across the earth in authenticity. Until enough people wake up to the level of loving self-awareness of their true authenticity, we're going to be stuck in the current cycles of violence and cruelty. Only when we can truly end violence against ourselves, will we no longer have violence in the world.

I call authenticity a power because one person simply being authentic will change the world and all of human creation. Being authentic is such a radical act of freedom, it creates ripple effects that are subtly felt throughout every interaction. Just as one act of kindness can create a wave of kindness through a community, so too can an act of true authenticity. The revolution is at hand. This revolution doesn't require violence or us to all organize together. It simply requires us to be ourselves and trust our true nature.

It's important to live as if we matter and mean something. Even though our bodies are but stardust decaying before the vast winds of time, we must act as if everything we do is vital.[4] Everything we do will fade away like sandcastles before an ocean wave. All that we do is simultaneously futile and matters so much. When we hold this paradox

---

[4] "Our bodies really are made of stardust" is a poetic way of saying the scientific truth. Currently, modern science understands that nearly all matter in the universe was made inside of the stars. According to an article on Michigan State University's website, the current theory of the formation of the universe is as follows. "In the Beginning There Were Three Elements": hydrogen, helium, and a little bit of lithium. All the other elements on the periodic table come from the stars.

in our hearts, I believe we can find the right balance between serious action and laughing at the strange, sad joke of existence.

All that we do is futile in the sense that we are extremely small forces compared to the stars. Even a star is just one of many millions upon millions of other stars. Even if we revolutionize the planet in love, how much will this love revolution affect the whole universe? Earth is just one planet among so many planets. Just as we look down on the insignificance of a single ant, so too could the stars look down on us.

Understanding the futility of our existence helps us not take ourselves too seriously. It's essential that we care and open our hearts so we don't fall into hopelessness. Every ant matters as every human matters, and so too does every star. The art of embodied wisdom is to live like every action is vital to all of creation while knowing at the same time it is just a small thing.

The revolution in the human heart starts with authenticity and it starts inside of you right now. Perhaps it has already begun long ago. You were born to be yourself. Completing your life's mission hinges on this authenticity. This is why authenticity starts with simply being yourself.

1 Be Yourself

The immense power of authenticity is in simply being yourself. Being authentic is what we are meant to be. We do not have to study with a teacher or spend years in practice to be authentic. It is what is here underneath all the airs and facades we might sometimes put on. When we strip away all that is not us, we are left with the naked truth of our authenticity.

We were all born with a unique set of gifts to share with the world. These gifts are our powers. Alongside these gifts, we also carry our wounds. The traumas of shame have touched us all. In our darker moments, each of us feels that we are not adequate to meet the challenges of life. Perhaps we are afraid that our life's mission is too big for us to complete. Perhaps in our darker moments we believe that there's something fundamentally wrong with us. It's easy to dismiss many of our small successes and acts of love. The standards of success set by society and our upbringing are often projections, which we are not meant to achieve. The challenge in authenticity is to meet the demands of life by staying true to what is inside of you.

The essayist, poet, and transcendentalist Ralph Waldo Emerson speaks about this when he says, "To be yourself in a world that is constantly trying to make you something else is the greatest accomplishment."[5] Emerson recognized the deep truth and power of authenticity. Authenticity is powerful because inscribed within each of us are instructions for how to meet every moment. This guidance system is greater than any technology possible. It's the wisdom right here inside our hearts. This intuitive wisdom is a treasure trove of insights waiting to come to light this very moment.

When we accept ourselves just as we are right now, we honor the authentic self that we truly are. This acceptance allows us to meet life with open and loving arms. Simply being yourself is the greatest act of courage you will ever perform. And the ironic thing is that it requires no pretense or desire to perform. It is simply what happens naturally when nothing else is in the way.

---

[5] From the book, *Ralph Waldo Emerson Essays*.

Story: *Being Myself*

I've always had a gift for supporting people through challenges. For years, I apprenticed with other teachers to study their methods. This was a very important phase for me to train with and experience how other people offer support and guidance in personal growth work. In some of my studies, I got lost believing others were better at this than me and I should imitate their style. I tried to copy their style. My longtime mentor encouraged me to be like him rather than follow my authentic way. When I individuated from him, I found I always knew the way I was meant to support people. It was right here in my heart all along. I was much like Dorothy in the *Wizard of Oz*. The power to return home was with her all along, yet she needed to go on the journey to discover the answers were always inside herself.

The hero's journey that Joseph Campbell's work focuses on rings true for all of us. We are on our own hero's journey to find ourselves and realize our potentials and gifts in life. Whatever way we go, we have the potential to awaken ourselves just as Odysseus did in Homer's *Odyssey*, and Frodo & Samwise did in Tolkien's *Lord of the Rings* series. Embrace your hero's journey by being yourself.

Straight Words: *Be Yourself*

Be yourself just as the wind, the sun, and the rain are themselves. There's nothing you need to strive to do or accomplish. Let yourself be content in who you are. When you find your ease in being yourself, you've found your natural resting place.

Game: *Be Yourself*

1. Notice your breath. Allow your breath to naturally become easier and more spacious.

2. Touch your heart and center your awareness in your heart.

3. Notice how your heart is the center of life. Feel its beat guiding you.

4. Allow yourself to be at ease just as you are. Nothing needs to change. There's nothing you need to push or accomplish.

5. Simply rest in the truth that you are yourself. There's nowhere to get to and nothing you need to do to be more yourself.

6. Allow your heart's love to flow freely to you. Embrace all that you are with this love.

2 *The Heart of the Heart*

Being authentic puts us squarely in relationship with our hearts. Finding the heart is easy if we can access our feelings. Feelings are the doorway to the heart. They call us home and return us to who we are meant to be. I underestimated my authenticity for years. Trying to be like others, I didn't realize I had a unique gift already here inside of me.

In my work supporting others in their process, I've also found that everyone has a unique gift that needs love and encouragement. One of my new friends is exceptionally good at sensing other people. However, through her experience and traumas, she has learned to take her perceptions personally as if they are about her. I've found her to be extremely accurate at reading others. The issue is when she filters life through her own insecurities, it's difficult for her to clearly see and treasure her gifts. I repeatedly encourage her to accept herself and treasure what she already has.

When we've lost touch with our heart, all we have to do is say, "I'm out of touch with my heart," or "I feel lost." It can feel vulnerable to admit the truth, yet in the act of being authentic we find our heart again. If what you seek is heart-centered living, then simply be yourself in everything you do, say, and think. When you are yourself, there's no effort at all. The doors that need to be opened for you will magically open.

Story: *Samantha's Authentic Heart*

Samantha is one of the most authentic people I know. Coming into the CEO position at Bridging Worlds Behavioral Services, has not been easy.[6] When she was first learning the financial aspect of the company, she got very stressed. Initially she felt shame. When she simply and courageously spoke to what she was feeling and experiencing, the shame vanished. By expressing what she felt, she immediately came back into balance. It's amazing how refreshing authenticity is. When we speak the truth, it immediately clears the situation. Often simply being aware of the truth may be enough to shift many situations. Sometimes speech or action can be what brings us into balance.

Straight Words: *Just be Real*

There's nothing more needed. Just stay true to who you really are and be real. This is the heart of the heart. Admit what you feel. Be honest with yourself. Tell the hard truths to yourself and others. This will ground you in everything you do.

------

[6] Bridging Worlds is the company I founded in 2012 to work with autistic and disabled youth and adults in Sonoma County, California. If interested, visit our website: bridgingworldsbehavioralservices.com.

Game: *The Heart of the Heart*

1. If you feel out of touch with your heart or a little off center, start by touching your heart.

2. Be honest with yourself about what *exactly* you feel. What are you noticing?

3. Say to yourself what you are noticing or experiencing.

4. Notice how it feels as you connect more deeply with the messages of your heart. This honesty can often bring you back in touch with your heart.

5. Keep being honest whenever you lose touch with your heart throughout the day. Let your feelings take you back to the truth of your heart.

6. If you only do this one exercise, you will have the essence of the whole book. When you lose connection with your heart, come back home.

7. Live from your heart by being aware of your feelings and in loving connection with your experience.

8. Enjoy your heart connection and return to it as often as you feel guided.

3 Committing to the Truth

Authenticity means staying connected to the truth of your being as it is unfolding in the moment. When we are true to ourselves, all of life opens for us. How do we know when we are true to ourselves and when we are not? We can spot inauthenticity in the following ways. Inauthenticity feels stressed, forced, and contrived—spurring us to create a false identity. Inauthenticity feels defended or closed. When we are authentic, we are solidly centered in our hearts. Inauthenticity feels out of resonance with what is happening in the moment.

If you take a close look, you'll notice that all inauthenticity comes from unconscious fear. Even those who consciously engage in manipulation are only doing so because they are afraid. If someone wasn't afraid, they wouldn't have any need to manipulate. They would simply be themselves.

When there's only raw, authentic, naked truth in the moment, there can be no imposter. We were all born into this world naked. We put layers of clothing over our true, authentic, naked selves. Clothing is beautiful and can be an artistic expression of who we are while it keeps us warm. And, there's nothing more beautiful than who we are underneath all the clothing and facades. If you are lucky enough to have a lover with whom you can be real, you can take off all of your armor, facades, and clothing to be your raw and naked self. This is the best way to make love. Being emotionally naked is also the best way to be in friendships, family, or at work if we are lucky enough to have a job where we can be real.

I dream of a culture where we can be authentic, at work, at home, at play, and in community. This dream is a revolution in the sense that it's so dramatically different from the way things are done right now. It's a radical change. I call this dream, Heart-Centered Revolutions, a revolution in being. It's not a revolution in which we mobilize in the streets and organize. It's a revolution in which we follow our hearts. The heart is the center of our being. Our being is naturally revolutionary when we are authentic. The authentic being casts off the shackles that have held humanity down for eons. When you stop thinking about your actions, they will arise from the core of your being without effort by the conscious will. This was described in great detail in the *Tao Te Ching* by Lao Tzu.

Story: *Authentic Greatness and Ease*

Being authentic is like entering the state of body awareness that a great athlete or dancer achieves when right action flows effortlessly from their being.[7] Basketball legend Michael Jordan is one of the greatest examples I've observed of this effortless action. His moment to moment ease and grace expresses his true nature and natural way of being. The way he would dribble, jump, spin, soar through the air, and shoot the ball inspired everyone who was watching. If you've never seen Michael Jordan play basketball, I suggest you look him up and admire the way he danced across the court. He was truly masterful. I always rooted against him and wanted the other teams to have a chance to win. Even though I didn't like him at the time, I couldn't help but appreciate his true greatness.

Straight Words: *Commit to Truth*

Being yourself is a living embodiment of truth. Commit to the truth of your nature. Truth creates ease. When we come from truth, there's no effort needed. There's no need to try to make ourselves different. We can be as we are and everything unfolds from this place. Be true to yourself always and in all ways. When you are not true to yourself, use these times as learning opportunities. Being kind and loving to ourselves is essential.

---

[7] This idea comes from Stephen Mitchell's introduction to his translation of the *Tao Te Ching*.

Embodying this kindness, we do not beat ourselves up for being who we are and this is the greatest gift we can give ourselves. We can learn so much more through the ease and grace of loving self-acceptance.

Game: *Truth Telling*

1. Practice telling the truth with someone who will be open to hearing you. Start with a trusted friend.

2. First connect with your heart. Touch your heart with your hand. Notice what you are really feeling in this moment. What are you experiencing?

3. Tell your trusted friend the simple truth of what you are feeling and experiencing right now without any embellishments or edits.

4. Notice what happens when you speak the truth.

5. Notice the power in the dynamic when you say what is true for you and are heard and witnessed in it.

6. Be open to the other's truth as well.

4 *Unconditional Love*

When we are guided by unconditional love, we are as we are. To be honest with yourself, true acceptance of your level of self-awareness and maturity is necessary. Trying to be ahead of yourself or trying in any way to be different than you are is the affliction that plagues the human race. These conditioned behaviors have infected humanity and have made us almost unrecognizable from who we really are. Without trying to rush ahead or be more mature than we are, we let ourselves *be* as we *are*. In this way we find true authenticity.

Story: *Unconditional Love and Authenticity*

When I was trying to be someone else, I didn't accept myself as I was. Now that I am letting myself be myself, my life is so much easier. I'm a very intense person with strong feelings. When I get mad it's because something is out of balance. My anger always tells me when something is out of balance. This was true when I was child. I would get mad at the injustice in bullying by standing up to cruel people. When I was a teenager, I got mad and spoke up when people were being discriminated against. I've always become angry when love is not honored. When I used to try to change my anger and not be so mad, I would beat myself up for what I was feeling. I would hold my feelings down and tolerate injustice.

Now I accept my anger as a gift from my heart. I've learned that acting from anger unconsciously is often imbalanced. But listening to the voice of anger helps me understand the profound truths I have been overlooking. Through accepting my anger, I lead my company in a way that is more attentive to the needs of the whole. Before, I was cutting myself off from my heart by judging my feelings. Having unconditional love for where I am makes everything so much easier and my life flows that much better. It puts my heart at the very center of everything I do.

Straight Words: *Stop Pretending*

The time for pretending is over. Love yourself and be as you are. There's no need to try to be different from how you are. Only when you love yourself as you are can you be truly authentic.

Game: *Authenticity*

There are many games in this book. If you only have the bandwidth to practice a few of them, explore this one along with the practice found in chapter two. You can use this one over and over, as much as you desire.

1. Get in touch with your heart. You can put your hand on your chest and touch it, or simply feel into and open your heart.

2. Allow your heart to lead your actions, words, and thoughts. The heart is always authentic. It stays true to all of your feelings and is true to what is right for your whole being.

3. What does the heart feel? Identify in a word or two exactly how your heart feels right now.

4. What does the heart want? Say to yourself one thing that the heart wants at this moment.

5. Be completely honest with yourself about where you are. You don't have to like it, just be true to it.

6. Continue on with your day from this place of authenticity centered in your heart.

7. Listen to your words and feel for how honest they are. Notice any places where you are hiding out of shame and just let this be present. When you are truly authentic, there's nothing you need to hide. You don't need to

reveal everything either. Simply share what you want from your heart in the moment.

8. Notice how much easier life is when you are authentic.

9. Keep being authentic for as long as you live by finding the subtle places where you are inauthentic. Every time you are aware of inauthenticity and choose to act more authentic, you refine your practice. Through this practice you can become more true to yourself every day in every possible way.

5 *Acceptance*

Acceptance is essential to authenticity. Authenticity is being true to who you are and where you are in the circumstances of your life. It may not be pretty, it may not be balanced, and it may not be a whole set of things, but it is just where you are. Acceptance is the healing balm that comes over us when we embody this kind of self-honesty.

Honesty and authenticity are nearly interchangeable. Authenticity is a state of being in which you are honest. Honesty is what describes a quality in your speech when you speak the truth. When you are honest, you become authentic. You can't be authentic without being honest. Authentic people honor the way of truth and strive to be as honest as possible. We must not compromise our authenticity, even given the pressures within the corrupt state of this world.

If you are with someone who is incapable of hearing your truth, or you find yourself in a situation in which telling the whole truth will compromise the highest good, it's okay to follow your heart and trust yourself to share as much or as little as is right to share. We never have to force ourselves to say anything. Being authentic is sharing as much as we feel moved to share in our hearts at the moment. Self-acceptance is the force that powers all authenticity. Without self-acceptance, it is very difficult to be authentic. If I had to choose just one prayer for all of humanity, I would choose a prayer of self-acceptance for all of us.

Story: *My Father Embodied Self-Acceptance*

My father was always true and honest. He had a remarkable and natural presence. My mother referred to him as having a "natural zen." He did not practice meditation or spirituality, but peace would often emanate from him. Yet, his zen was not always peaceful.

When my father felt disrespected by another parent at one of my little league baseball games, he was forthright and honest with the other parent. He was not ashamed to be angry; he was as he was. When another parent was disrespectful to my father based on my father's Indian ethnicity, my father confronted the man and did not kowtow to the man's bigotry. He took a stand for what he believed.

He brought this same authenticity to his profession. While my father taught law school, he was pressured to dumb down and simplify the material for the newer wave of students who wanted to be spoon fed. My father kept teaching in a way that was true to his being. He did not bow to the changing times. He stayed true to his code and taught from his authenticity. Even though the administration wanted him to change, he honored his ideals about quality teaching and learning over what anyone else wanted from him. This style of teaching led him to be one of the most popular and well-loved teachers at Seton Hall Law School in the 70s and 80s, and widely disliked in the 2000s when students expected more structure. My father didn't really care about the change in his popularity. He stuck to his guns. He showed us how to roll with the self-acceptance that resides in our hearts.

Straight Words: *Be True and Accept*

Let go of all this petty politeness and be true to the movements of your heart. Don't succumb to the pressure to be different from who you are. Be completely honest and naked with yourself. You have nothing left to hide. You are as you are. Be yourself. Accept yourself.

Game: *Play with Inauthenticity to Find Acceptance*

1. Play with being intentionally inauthentic to yourself. Try to make yourself different from how you are.

2. Force yourself to be a certain way for a couple of seconds or a minute. One easy way to do this is to pick a person you admire and try to mold yourself to be like them.

3. Make yourself think in a way that's not true to you, or create a rule in your mind that doesn't feel like how you want to act. You might try saying, "I should be more focused or less distracted," or "I should love waking up early."

4. Every time you act like yourself instead of the way you've prescribed yourself to act, get mad at yourself and make yourself try to be different. Beat yourself up psychologically for not doing a good enough job. You can literally start yelling at yourself in your head, "I'm so stupid. I should be more aware or better at communicating."

5. Have fun and exaggerate the trying, like you are acting on stage with some of your own patterns. Try as hard as you can to be different from how you are.

6. Experience the absurdity of this exercise. Notice how it feels in your body to try and make yourself different. This game will help you recognize the absurdity of the critical

voice in your head telling you to be other than you are.

7. Now stop trying to be different and allow yourself to simply be.

8. You don't need to fix or change anything. Your awareness and natural state is fine just the way it is.

9. Notice how it feels when the pressure and demands of being a certain way have been lifted from your heart.

10. How do you prefer to be? Do you like to allow your natural state to lead, or do you prefer to force yourself to be different? The choice is entirely up to you. The path of ease is always best. Be yourself! Accept yourself.

6 Being Raw

Authenticity is not shy and it doesn't mince words. It simply is itself. It says what it has to say. Some people may take offense at authenticity, but that's because they put their egos in front of the truth. When we honor the truth, we honor the way of authenticity in others even if their authenticity bruises our egos. This truth telling comes straight from the heart. In fact, the fastest way to connect with your heart is to simply be authentic. Our hearts are always raw and authentic.

Story: *Being Raw and True to the Heart*

After I had helped many of my friends out of the cult, I found that they were continuing to judge each other with the same kind of energy the leader of the cult had embodied. I was deeply triggered by judgmental energy at this time. Whenever anyone embodied judgmental energy around me, I was raw and true to my heart. Linda, one of the members of the group, tried to tell me that I was being like the cult leader. I said, "No. I'm following the authentic truth of the heart." She and many others were convinced that I was being unloving. I was simply being completely naked with how I felt with them in each moment. Many of them couldn't handle my directness. Yet it was where my heart was. I'm glad I followed and spoke the raw authentic truth of my heart.

Embodying this raw, naked truth helped filter the people out of my life who were in a different vibration from me. I'm grateful for the profound realness of my heart. My friends and social circle began to match the new level of self-acceptance and love I was finding.

Straight Words: *Come from the Heart*

The heart is direct and clear. It knows what it knows and wants what it wants. When you come from the heart, you have the most direct channel to truth and love. Feel your heart, know its rhythms, and open your heart to the direct truth. You know how to do this. Just remember where you came from and who you really are!

You don't have to be wise beyond your years or ahead of yourself. The heart always knows what is right for the moment for your learning path. Trust the naked and raw truth that comes from the heart.

Game: *Come From the Heart*

1. Smile and playfully get in touch with your heart.

2. Place your hand on your heart. Breathe and center your awareness here.

3. As you breathe, notice how your connection with your feelings deepens. The more deeply you feel, the more you get in contact with your heart.

4. How does your heart feel? Notice the subtle sensations in your heart. Is it tight or loose? Warm or cool? Hard or soft? Moving or still? Light or heavy? [8]

5. If the feelings in your heart had words, what would they say? Let the words come forward and tune into them. The heart has so much wisdom to share with us.

6. Simply notice and allow whatever comes.

7. Your heart can be the center of all your actions. Be honest with what you are feeling right now. Just allow and love yourself as you are.

8. Send some love to your beautiful and authentic heart.

---

[8] This series of questions was developed by John Pateros, the founder of Process Coaching. In many of the exercises I use these questions to get in touch with body sensations. When we are aware of the body sensations, self-awareness comes much more easily.

7 *Unlearning*

Authenticity cannot be taught. When inauthenticity is unlearned or let go of, authenticity is what replaces it. No one can show you how to be you. Your own organic way of being emerges naturally from yourself. Others can feel when you are closer to your essence if they know you well. But you must always discern for yourself what is truly you.

You can open the door for authenticity with your intention, but it happens like the Sun rises—naturally and effortlessly. It's a spontaneous and unplanned happening. When you are yourself, the magic of your life fully happens. You can help remove obstacles to authenticity. You can help inspire it, but you cannot copy another person and be authentic. You must find your own unique way of being.

Story: *Can't Help But Be Himself*

I work with autistic and developmentally disabled clients. In my experience, autistic and developmentally disabled people are often much more authentic than neurotypical people. One of my clients is a male in his early 20s who always tells me exactly where he is and what is happening for him. Sometimes he does it through his poetry, and other times he says exactly what he does not feel like doing. I've even seen him walk away when he doesn't want to participate in what's going on. It doesn't matter what is happening, he just knows how to be completely authentic with who he is. No one ever taught him how to do it. He just does it as naturally as the Sun rises.

Straight Words: *Authenticity Can Not be Taught*

No one else knows better than you about how to be you. You are the one who gets to decide how to be. You know everything you need to know to be yourself and fulfill your destiny. You came into this world with instructions inscribed in your heart. Trust these instructions, and be open to what you really feel. There is no class or teacher who can show you how to be. These instructions live inside your heart and soul. Unlock them. Open to your destiny.

Game: *Unlearning*

This is the game we always longed to play at school when instead we had to conform.

1. Think about everything you know about how to be a human being in this world.

2. Make a list in your mind of all the ways you are supposed to be as a human being. (It could be patient, understanding, motivated, loving, etc.)

3. Let it all go, like you're flushing a toilet. Simply let go of any preconceptions you have about how you are supposed to be as you breathe out.

4. Notice what happens as you inhale. Continue breathing and observing.

5. Notice the stress that comes from clinging to expectations. Notice how it feels in your body.

6. Whenever you want, you can simply breathe out any conditioning or belief about how you are supposed to be. Breathe in and allow yourself to be as you are.

7. As you breathe out, continue letting go of anything you believe that is limiting. Now, allow yourself to be the way you were meant to be.

8. What does it feel like when you allow yourself to simply be as you are, as natural as a plant or animal?

9. There's no need for all this extra thinking and worrying. You are nature. Simply be at ease with yourself.

10. As you move through your day and through your life, keep playing this game in the background of your awareness.

8 Be True To Yourself

"To thine own self be true," comes from William Shakespeare's play *Hamlet* which has withstood the test of time. Polonius gives advice to his son who is leaving for university, telling him, "This above all: to thine own self be true." Authenticity is always being true to oneself. That's the very definition of authenticity.

Story: *How I Became True to Myself*

When I was seven, I remember my father debating about legalizing drugs. He was in a room full of people who staunchly disagreed with him. Rather than react or conform, he calmly and confidently backed up all of his arguments with clear logic, passion, and evidence.

He fought against racism and exposed the fallacy of viewing people by skin color. He defined race as a social construct rather than an inherent quality. We could just as easily categorize people by nose size instead of skin color. He railed against all sorts of conventions. He would even fart out loud in front of other people. He didn't do any of these things to prove a point. He simply was not ashamed of his bodily functions and did not heed the manners of the society. I remember one time when he farted in front of my high school friends. Even though it was fairly embarrassing for me as a teenager, it taught me to not care about what others think and to simply be true to myself. The way he trusted his sense of rightness became part of my own backbone. I've had to learn to stand on my own authority. He raised me well and helped me to do this.

My father's authority was in the realm of thinking. My authority is in the realm of feeling. I have always had a strong intuitive sense of what was happening. I trust my feelings about something over what others may say. I've learned this trust through many experiences in which I trusted what others said over my own feelings. Every time I've doubted my gut feelings, I've found out later that they were right. After enough experience, I've learned to listen to myself and what feels right for me.

I have a lot of confidence in the areas where I perceive things more clearly than many others. I've been called arrogant by many people. I used to believe that they were right. As I've come to know myself better, I don't believe I was ever arrogant. When I feel someone is being even the slightest bit divisive or hostile, I trust my feelings. I have found that these small feelings give me clues about disconnections in the field of the interaction.

When I use the word field, I am referring to the energetic container of the space between and around each of us in an interaction. It can be described as the sense you have when you intuitively feel a dynamic. Subtle divisiveness is part of what happens in many connections.

I have more space and patience for these subtle patterns of behavior now that I'm trusting myself. When I was first learning to speak up for myself, I needed everyone around me to agree with my perceptions. This created a lot of conflict. Now I don't need others to agree with me, they just need to have space for my feelings and thoughts. This is what we naturally offer each other when we use empathy in our communications.

Straight Words: *Be True to You*

It doesn't matter what anyone else thinks of you. In fact, their thoughts about you have more to do with them than you unless they are good at empathy. When you find the truth in your heart to live from, you've found your guiding star to follow. Stand true to your heart. Stand true to yourself.

Don't let anyone sway you or give you a negative attitude about yourself from their false opinions and judgments. It's always good to be open to others' perceptions of you and learn from them. Even divisive people will help you see yourself more clearly if you filter out the negativity and find any truth in their perceptions. Almost every vantage point has at least a hint of truth in it. However, be aware that when people are projecting strongly onto you, there will be nearly no truth in it for you. They are simply revealing the truth of their own judgmental mind. Truly authentic people are loving and have empathy for others. Judgmental people will often claim they are being authentic as an excuse to express their hatred and condemnation. For example, a person embodying racism and bigotry can express a hateful view of another race and simply say they are being authentic. Authenticity feels good to an open heart. Judgment, condemnation, and hatred hurts an open heart.

Game: *Be True to Yourself*

1. Pretend you're on a mission from God, the Universe, or whatever force guides everything for you.

2. Listen to every word that you say. Notice when there is anything untrue in what you say.

3. Watch your actions closely and find anything that seems false or untrue.

4. Keep refining your words and actions, so that everything you do comes from the very core of your being.

5. Realize that this isn't really a game you're making up. It's your deepest mission—the game at the very fabric of creation.

6. When you are true to yourself, you put yourself on the fast track to fulfill your destiny. Keep being true to yourself and notice what unfolds.

9 We Are All Amazingly Large

Who we are is amazingly large. The conditioning of our world would have us believe we are ordinary. Each one of us is extraordinary. We are all like stars in the night sky. We are meant to shine our unique gifts into this world. We are a microcosm which contains everything in the universe. Thinking we are small has been one of the greatest traps to our authenticity.

I've looked to inspirational leaders of the past to help me along the way as I take back my authentic power and realize how truly large I am. Nelson Mandela famously quoted Mary Ann Williamson in one of his speeches:

> Our deepest fear is not that we are inadequate. Our deepest fear is that we are powerful beyond measure. It is our light, not our darkness that most frightens us. We ask ourselves, 'Who am I to be brilliant, gorgeous, talented, fabulous?' Actually who are you not to be. You are a child of god. Your playing small does not serve the world... We are all meant to shine.

Rumi says, "Stop acting so small. You are the universe in ecstatic motion." Walt Whitman's iconic poem "Songs of Myself" goes, "Dazzling and tremendous how quick the sun-rise would kill me, if I could not now and always send sun-rise out of me. We also ascend dazzling and tremendous as the sun."

When we embrace the teachings of great poets and mystics, we know we are the universe in its expression. We are not small and petty. We are large beyond all measure.

Story: *Mistaken Ego*

I was in deep meditation when a thought came through in my mind, *I'm really good at meditation.* I have been trained to detect egoic thoughts, and this one had every characteristic of a typical egoic thought. I rejected the thought and said to myself, "You're filled with ego today." But something didn't fully feel right. So I sat with it longer, and eventually realized that the thought *I'm good at meditation* was organically arising from my being.

I strive to look at myself objectively. It's like looking at a good friend who I love dearly and am wanting to be completely honest with. This is the kind of objectivity I strive for. A loving objectivity that is brutally honest. In that meditation, I realized how much the thoughts of being small and playing small had been holding me back. There's a kind of authenticity in seeing our immense gifts! I am good at altered states. I'm gifted with feeling. I've always been great at perceiving the truth. I do not mean this as bragging. I could tell you all the things I'm not good at too, like matching pitches with my voice, rhythm, or spelling. There are many things I'm challenged by in this life. Recognizing the truth of the heart has always been a gift of mine. When I've been mistaken and misperceived the truth, it is easy for me to own it and take responsibility.

Game: *The Vastness*

1. Touch your heart and center your awareness here.

2. Notice that your awareness extends out to your whole body.

3. Notice the air that is touching your skin or the ground beneath your feet.

4. Extend your awareness out into the air around you and ground beneath you.

5. Look around and notice what you see.

6. What if your sense of self extends into everything you perceive? It's as if you are part of everything you perceive.

7. Experience your vastness expanding and raying out beyond your body.

8. You are a vast and powerful being. Feel the fullness of this vastness.

9. Carry this with you as you move through your day.

10 Love is the Basic Fact

Love is. Love is an authentic, real, and soulful yes to experience the fullness of this life. Love helps us to savor every last ounce of life while we have it. We won't always be here in this form. We won't always be experiencing the ones we are with currently. Love is the raw basic fact of our existence when we strip away all that is not love.

Love is not some grand gesture of admiration or adoration. It simply is what we feel towards life and the universe if we are truly open in our heart and soul. Let's make the most of it and be as outrageous and lovingly authentic as we possibly can in this short time we have to dance upon the earth.

Story: *Authentic Love*

My mother is named Janet Bulbulia, and she is one of the most loving people I know. She certainly has her issues and flaws, but the way she nurtured me as a parent was exquisite. She tended to my needs where I didn't know I had them. She supported me in ways that continue to help me blossom into life. She got organic foods, shielded me from sugar and excessive technology, and nurtured my health deeply.

My mother's love is most profoundly characterized by her insistence that I was a good student in high school. I didn't want to work hard to get good grades. I just wanted to cruise, get by, and have fun. She made sure I was in honors and advanced placement classes. She spoke to teachers and advocated for me in every way she could. She made sure I wrote good essays and studied hard for my tests.

I fought her because I wanted her to just let me be and not push me. But she was right. Her insistence on me being a good student was a deep recognition of my potential. She supported me to get into Dartmouth College and fulfill my greater destiny. I wouldn't have been able to write books in my 40s without her pushing me and nurturing my potential at a young age. To this day, her love is an inspiration to me and all my work.

Straight Words: *True Love is Unconditional*

Love can't be conditional and also true. Love must be unconditional or don't go near it. When our "love" is based on conditions, it is selfish and possessive which often comes from fear. This is not love. True love is eternal. It cannot be eclipsed by anything, including the passage of time or crappy behavior from the other person. True love is not self-sacrificing. True love authentically looks out for the good of everyone involved. True love serves the potential inside all people. It ends all divisions and unites us all. I'm so grateful I have my mother's unconditional love.

Game: *Love is All There Is*

1. Put your hand on your heart. Open to the love that's here.

2. Let go of anything that's in the way of your heart and feel your heart pulsing under your hand.

3. Let go of any worries about the future or thoughts of the past. Get present right here and now.

4. Simply breathe in and out. There is only this moment to be in.

5. Notice the love that is here underneath everything when you are relaxed. It's the feeling of ease and 'okayness' with things just as they are.

6. Open to this love for yourself and life. Let it fully be alive in your heart and in your being.

7. Celebrate this love that you are.

11 Born Innocent and True

We are all born innocent and true. As I understand it, there's no foul or inherently evil soul here on this planet. There are forces which try to influence human beings. When we are lost in trauma, we can easily become taken over by dark forces.

Evil is a loaded word with many meanings. I define evil as the forces that cause separation and disconnection inside the human being. Evil goes beyond simply being unconscious. Evil requires malicious intent. Evil is a temporary state of imbalance that humans or spirits may find themselves in. Evil is not ultimately or irrevocably bad. However, when we come from evil we have a conscious or unconscious intent to hurt another and be divisive.

By returning to the authentic state we were born into, we naturally return to innocence and truth. Innocence lies in a newborn baby's eyes. It's here inside each one of our tender hearts. Whenever we open our heart, we return to the soft state of innocence we came in with at birth.

Story: *A Tale of Innocence*

Every baby is born crying, naked, helpless, and open. If you've ever been a part of a birth, you know the innocence and purity that newborns have. As Martin Luther King Jr. said, "Babies… are the latest news from heaven."[9] We are born into this world as innocent babies in our parents' arms. As babies, we are teeming with so much hope and potential. Do you remember your birth or the birth of a baby you watched enter the world? Remember the original innocence of this experience.

Straight Words: *We are Innocent*

It's time to stop believing in the lies of false religion or any twisted philosophy which says human nature is bad. Obviously there's evil in the world. It's plain as day to see the evil in our economy, in the way we treat each other when we drive, and the cruelty expressed on social media. There's a careless selfishness underneath the foundation of this society that is designed to hurt and oppress others.

Even though we are born good and innocent, the potential for evil lives inside the human soul. We have to be capable of either good or evil to have

---

[9] Martin Luther King Jr. expressed this in response to the killing of innocent black children.

good. If we are only good without the capacity for evil, we are like robots of the good without being truly free.

Some might find original innocence and evil in contradiction. I do not. The capacity to do great evil is part of our original innocence. We are born open to all forces. We are open to the forces of good and the forces of evil. We are open to all potential or we cannot be truly free. A truly free person never acts from evil. They appreciate and consider evil possibilities, but choose to never act from evil. If we find ourselves acting in a cruel way toward others, we must first accept ourselves. This cruelty is a result of traumas that have been passed down to us. Accepting ourselves as we are allows us to return to innocence.

I have never met a person who didn't have the innocence of a child inside their heart and soul. No matter how buried it may be, all people are capable of great love and compassion. We are all good and innocent underneath bad conditioning.

Game: *Return to Innocence*

1. Remember your own birth. The story is inside the cells of your body. (It may help to hear the story of your birth from your parents if you don't know it. Oftentimes parents don't talk

to children about the traumas of birth unless they are directly asked.)

2. Go back in time to the point before your conscious memory and access the time when you first entered this world from the other world.

3. You'll know you are here because there was an original innocence which preceded any notion of being bad. Your true nature is good.

4. Feel this goodness deep within your body.

5. Society is often run by evil forces. The game is to fight the evil forces with the love of your open and innocent heart. Remember the goodness that you are born from and that you feel.

6. Open your heart to your eternal and untouchable innocence.

7. If you want, play the song "Return to Innocence" by Enigma, a German band, and remember your original innocence.

Game: *Remember the Other's Innocence*

1. Remember that everyone you interact with was once a baby. Take someone you can't

stand who really pisses you off or acts in an
unconscious way.

2.　Remember that they were once a newborn
and innocent baby coming into the world.

3.　Imagine their birth. Imagine some of the
traumas they may have experienced. Perhaps
they had birth trauma. Perhaps their parents
were fighting, addicts, died young, abandoned
them, or were lost in hatred. Perhaps they
were not loved in the ways they needed to be
loved in order to live life with an open heart.
Maybe they were abused physically, sexually,
or emotionally.

4.　Whatever the reason is, something caused
them to be lost in their trauma.

5.　Open your heart with compassion to them for
all that they are.

6.　Extend the love in your heart to them for
their innocence and beauty.

Note: You don't have to interact with this person;
they might be toxic to you. However, inwardly
you can always keep your heart open to them by
remembering their innocence.

12 Our Core is Creative

Our core essence is creative. Life is an art of manifesting. The more I get in touch with my authentic way of being, the more that comes out in my music, sculpture, writing, teaching, creativity in business, and conversations. When we are in touch with our being, our natural creativity blossoms forward.

Story: *Creativity Blossoms in Authenticity*

I never considered myself a very creative person. I was more of an athletic person growing up. Now I write books each day, compose songs, and sometimes make sculptures. The way I do business is creative. When I dropped into the truth of my being, I found I had always been creative. I just didn't know that I was. These abilities were inside of me all along, just like a fairy tale hero who goes on a journey to find out they already had everything they needed. I guess that's what our lives truly are—journeys to find our gifts.

Julia Cameron first taught me the connection between authenticity and creativity. Her practice of writing morning pages simply flushes out everything that you think on paper. In the process, you are completely authentic with the thoughts which come from your head onto the paper. The practice of automatic writing helped my creativity blossom more than any other practice. I'm grateful for this practice and her great book, *The Artist's Way*.

Straight Words: *We are All Creative*

We are all creative. You are an artist and you are meant to create. If you don't know this already, open your eyes and look around. Your life is your canvas. Your life is clay for your sculpture. How do you want to shape it? What colors do you want to paint with? What form or forms do you want to create? Notice the art you are already manifesting in your everyday life.

Game: *Creativity*

1. Get in touch with your creative impulse.

2. Notice what you feel moved to do that's creative. It might be to paint, dance, sing, play music, act, write, draw, sculpt, cook, knit, crochet, or something else unique to you.

3. Follow whatever creative inspiration that is moving inside of you.

4. In what form or medium do you want to express yourself? Start by jotting down some notes.

5. Follow your inspiration. Go create in whatever medium you prefer. Notice how it feels.

6. Let the creativity come from your true authentic being.

7. Don't judge what you create, simply let your creativity flow through you.

13 The Dangers of Manners

Manners often inhibit authenticity. Manners impose a set of rules that we must conform to in order to be acceptable in society. I'm defining manners as different from basic agreements of respect. Treating each other with respect and empathy is common courtesy. Not sneezing or coughing on each other is simply an act of kindness. Manners, however, are an imposed set of rules from the outside that predetermine which behaviors are okay and which are not okay.

For example, it is not acceptable to cry in public, or tell the truth if it hurts another person's feelings. Following these manners actually lead us to inauthenticity. Any manners that repress authentic feeling and authentic being should be seen for what they are—a set of lies used to control, condition, and manipulate us into not being ourselves. It's okay to be authentic in the face of conditioning. It's like disobeying a socially unconscionable law such as Apartheid, or any other discriminatory, unjust practice. We should challenge manners and any form of repression they may result in. It's always okay to be true to ourselves in the moment.

Story: *Authenticity Over Manners*

When I was a teenager, I was leaving the library with my friend André. An older lady in her 70's came up to me and said, "You shouldn't do that." I said, "Do what?" She replied, "You know what you did." I said, "No, I don't know. Please tell me!" As we kept going back and forth, I became progressively angrier at her for assuming that I knew what she was talking about when I did not.

For the record, I love elders. But I can't stand when people make assumptions and disrespect others. If she respected me, she would have told me what she believed I had done. I was a teenager. It's possible I was making too much noise for the library or having too much fun for the boundaries of the space.

On this particular day, we were quieter and more well behaved than usual. I really had no idea what she was talking about. Still to this day I don't really know if her point was valid since she never explained it. I believe André didn't know what she was talking about either. I suspect I must have unconsciously violated some manner of politeness.

Ironically, she was being very rude to me by not even telling me what the actual issue was. This is the kind of unnecessary crap that can happen when we're governed by manners and politeness instead of authenticity. All she had to understand was that I sincerely didn't know what she was talking about. She could have told me what she didn't like and perhaps I would have learned from her. I guess I learned more from her decision to withhold her perspective as I'm still carrying the lessons forward into this book over 30 years later. The injustice of it marked a significant occurrence in my memory. It helped me know as a teenager that when I got older, I would treat younger people with respect and dignity. I would never presume they should know what I'm talking about when they might not. This older lady had taught me the error of prioritizing manners over authenticity. I promised myself that I would never make the same mistake she made.

The greatest exemplar I know of bucking manners is Greta Thunberg. When I think about the way she addressed the leaders of the world at the UN Climate Summit in 2019 my heart is uplifted by her honesty and courage.

> How dare you. You have stolen my dreams and my childhood with your empty words... People are suffering. People are dying. Entire ecosystems are collapsing. We are

> in the beginning of a mass extinction, and all you can talk about is fairytales of money and eternal economic growth. How dare you.

I admire the authenticity and denial of traditional manners she embodied. Many criticized Greta for her tone and the way she spoke to the leaders. I deeply admire and respect her for it. The world leaders were and are still ignoring the climate crisis. I admire her fire, courage, and conviction. She is an example of authenticity that we may all strive to emulate.

Straight Words: *Heart is Beyond Manners*

Prioritizing manners over the heart engenders a subtle form of imbalance that I like to call evil. When we prioritize manners over heart, we prioritize the way we think we are supposed to be over the way we actually are. This is a cruel attack on our very own nature and that is why I call it evil. There's a malice in this attack on our being that goes beyond simple unconsciousness. When we trust in human nature, we trust in the heart and we do and say what's in our heart to do and say.

Game: *Letting Go of Manners that Don't Serve*

1. Notice all the manners you were taught as a child, like how to eat and how to talk in a way that is polite and civilized. (Some manners are good—the bathroom is where you relieve yourself, you wash your hands when they get dirty, and you make sure your shoes don't have mud on them when you go inside the house. These manners are prudent and don't restrict authenticity.)

2. Find a manner that represses authenticity. For example, "It's rude to say what you feel." Or, "You should always be nice."

3. Think about this manner and start trying to make yourself act from it. You might even exaggerate the use of this manner, as if all of your world now conforms to this manner. Notice the way it narrows your world.

4. Simply let go of this manner as you let your breath out. Breathe in the freedom to do whatever you really feel and want here.

5. Notice how good it feels to let go of the manner which entraps you.

6. Continue to spot any manners that repress your true freedom. Keep practicing this exercise throughout your day and your life.

14 The Authentic Being

When we are in touch with our being, all we can do is be authentic. What other way can we be? An animal or a plant is always authentic. They put on no facades. When a human being opens their heart, they can only be authentic. There's no other way to be other than the way we truly are in the moment.

Story: *The Authentic Deer*

At sunrise, I watch the deer who walk on the field outside my house. It's a family of five. They love to eat the grass and enjoy the start of the new day, just as I enjoy watching the sunrise. The deer are authentic. They do not put on any pretenses. They are as they are. They enjoy the outdoors and love to run. They get scared easily and are honest about it. They are authentic.

Straight Words: *Authenticity is True*

When we try to be authentic, we move away from authenticity. No trying is needed. Simply say what is true for you right now! What is in your heart right now? Authenticity is the most natural thing in the world, but it's not always easy. Being authentic is like swimming against the current of society. It's saying, "no matter what, I stay true to me." While authenticity is going upstream in regards to society, authenticity is swimming downstream with the forces of nature. Everything in nature is authentic. How can anything be but what it is? Observe nature being itself like the sun, a tree, or a deer. Embody your own nature. Be your radical, authentic self. What do you truly have to lose?

Game: *Being Authentic*

1. Notice what you are feeling right now.

2. If you are with another person, connect with the other person or people.

3. Simply speak the truth of what you are feeling. See what happens next.

4. If you are alone, simply honor what is in your nature to do. Now do only that.

5. When you allow your nature to lead, it's very easy. Just be as you are and do as you do.

6. Continue playing this authenticity game for as long as you live if you want. There's no good reason to ever stop playing.

15 Beyond Forms and Definition

When you define yourself, you confine yourself. To be truly authentic, you keep yourself free of any fixed definitions. You have values and elements that you are committed to, but you are not attached to any particular way of being other than being true to yourself. In this way, our beliefs become working hypotheses, which are always open for redefinition whenever a deeper layer of truth presents itself. Any forms that are confining can be cast off. Authenticity is an ever evolving form that is not stuck or fixed in one position. Instead, it keeps on unfolding itself as you learn, mature, and wisen.

Story: *When I Lost the Definition of Myself*

I used to know exactly who I was. One evening in New England I looked up at the stars and felt the oneness of all of life flow through me. The radiant fullness of life flooded through my heart. For a flash of time there was no distinction between me, the stars, and The Green of Dartmouth College. I was at one with all that I was perceiving. This experience defied the way I had defined myself as a separate being who didn't believe in a higher power. I was an atheist who believed in a material reality and I was experiencing something beyond my definition.

This experience was so strong it forever altered my perception of the universe. From that point on, I knew that my true nature was beyond any conception my mind could concoct. I'm a great mystery connected with the mystery of the stars, the earth, and the cosmos. I am as ancient as the original winds. It's been so liberating to embrace the undefined self of who I really am. This was my first spiritual awakening. It took me from being an atheist to being a mystic.

Straight Words: *Don't Define Yourself*

Defining yourself only confines you. Leave yourself open to evolving. It's okay to share truths you know about yourself. But don't get lost in the illusion of thinking you know who you are. We don't have a clue. Who we are is much deeper than anything we could ever say about ourselves or conceptualize in our limited mind.

Game: *Beyond Forms and Definitions*

1. Touch your heart and feel its rhythm. Sense how you feel about yourself and your life in this moment.

2. Where does your sense of self center? It may appear to be in your head as the head holds so many senses—sight, sound, smell and taste.

3. Move your head from side to side. Ask yourself, "Am I moving or is my head moving?"

4. Now move a finger from side to side. Notice how it is clear that your finger is moving, not your whole self.

5. Keep alternating between the finger and the head until you have the sense that it is only your head that is moving when your head moves rather than all of you.[10]

6. Notice that there is a sense of self beyond any specific point of the body.

---

[10] This is a tantric exercise as taught by Francis Lucille, a western teacher of the non-dual *Advaita* tradition. My friend Kenan taught me this simple practice.

7. Breathe in and out. As you exhale, let go of any sensory information you might be holding onto and return to the state of fundamental being.

8. Being is free-flowing. We are not limited by our thinking. Being is an experience of this moment outside of concepts. Feel the breath, feel the heart, and feel the sense of expansion.

9. You are not your body. You inhabit your body. It's good to treasure your body and treat it well. Remember that who you are is not fixed in time and space.

10. Feel the sense of the eternal inside of you. This is the truth of your authentic being.

11. Your body will die as all forms do. Your being is timeless and deathless.

16 Feelings vs. Thinking

Your feelings will often bring you closer to your authentic self than your thinking will. Your feelings guide you to who you really are. Your thinking can go in many directions, yet your feelings are always true. Feeling is not better than thinking. Feeling is deeper and closer to the core of our being, while thinking is closer to the surface of our being.

Sometimes the surface and superficial matters are judged against. But we live on the surface of the earth. We wouldn't survive in the core. Sometimes being on the surface is better. Yet when it comes to living from our being, the depth is typically best. This is why we want to connect to feelings. Feelings allow us to go deeper. Both thinking and feeling have different gifts. Once we honor the right place of feeling, we naturally come into balance.

Story: *Feeling*

The one place I have surpassed my father in authenticity is in the realm of the heart and feeling. He was way beyond me in his thinking capacity. His awareness of the law, politics, economics, and history was enormous. While he was acutely aware of his thinking, he was not very aware of his heart and feelings. He often had difficult dynamics with one of his sisters. He loved his whole family very much and it was difficult for him to have conflict in the family. He never understood why his sister took offense to his playful teasing.

He was the eldest brother, also known as *moti baji* (literally, "little father" in Gujarati, a language that originated in Western India where my family is from). I could see for myself how his sister never liked that kind of teasing interaction from him. She felt unfairly picked on, as younger siblings often do.

Later in my father's life, he sought my council to better understand the dynamic between the two of them. It was an honor to have him ask for my help. He was always a gifted teacher and didn't need help with many things. I was talking with my brother recently about my father when my brother said, "Dad wasn't a good communicator." I said, "He was not good at expressing his feelings, but he was an excellent communicator about his ideas. Remember when he talked about politics or law? He was always good at saying what he wanted to say."

Straight Words: *Feel for Who You Truly Are*

Feel for who you truly are. The authentic way is to live, let live, and allow. How many ways can I say it's okay to be yourself? When you feel who you are, you will only be yourself. Whatever is not you will not remain here inside you. Let it go. It's so much easier this way.

Game: *Underneath Every Thought Is A Feeling*

1. Take any thought you are having right now. It could be about what you are reading here, something that you thought earlier, or anything else that is up for you right now.

2. Imagine the thought is on the surface of a lake.

3. Feel for what's underneath this thought. What do you experience below the surface?

4. You will either find another thought or feeling. Keep asking yourself what is underneath this thought or feeling until you arrive at the core essence of what is underneath. You'll know you're at the core when you feel like you are at the bottom of something and there's no deeper place you can go.

5. When you arrive at a feeling, ask yourself, "Where do I feel it in my body?" Feel for where in your body this feeling centers. *Note:* Finding a sensation in the torso often helps us get out of our head and into the body more fully.

6. Is the feeling you've located in your torso tight or loose? Moving or still? Sharp or dull? Warm or cool? Soft or hard? Light or heavy?

7. Tune into this feeling and notice how your awareness deepens as you connect with this feeling underneath the thought.

8. Allow and accept the feeling as it is. Keep practicing feeling what is underneath your thinking as you go through your day. Feelings connect you directly to your experience. Open to them.

17 *Trying Comes From the Ego*

Trying is driven by the egoic mind. It's based on the belief that there's something inherently wrong with us. When we let go of all trying and striving, we can truly be ourselves. Free of any preconceived notion of who we should be, we can be how we actually are. Life is a strange game. We are born to be a certain way, and that way lives inside of us from the start. Society teaches us to avoid and deny this authentic way of being. Unless we challenge societal conditioning and learn to stay true to ourselves, we are trapped living by a set of rules which will only keep us chained to being different from who we naturally are.

Story: *Ego*

One of my friends and coworkers has been stuck in a pattern of trying to improve himself and be a better person. He's inflating himself with his ego to try to overcompensate for the deflation. We can only get out of the egoic pattern when we return to the size we actually are. The pattern of ego inflation and deflation is all too common in our world today. Self-acceptance means not trying to be any different than we are. It's often a momentous struggle to accept ourselves for who we really are.

This specific friend of mine has identified himself as a narcissist. Narcissistic patterns can be really hard to break out of even after we admit them to ourselves.

Straight Words: *Be Your Right Size*

Be your right size. Don't inflate or deflate. The truth is exactly how it is, no better or worse than that. It's no bigger or smaller than it is. In loving the ego, we can let go of identifying only with the ego. Anytime we try to avoid the ego, we actually become the ego. Only the ego would attempt to cut another part out. The being knows only love and wholeness. The being includes all our parts.

Game: *Loving the Ego*

1. Notice a place where you feel identified in your personal sense of self. It could be a story about what's not fair about life, what is hard, or a habitual way of clinging to your identity.

2. Notice that this place comes out of a state of ego identity.`

3. Touch your heart with your hand. Open to your deeper being. The deeper being is in touch with all of life and connected to the very heart of all things.

4. From this place of deeper being, open to the ego. Love all the things the ego is experiencing and let the ego know you're here.

5. Embrace all the worries and fears that may be present, and just allow the ego to be as it is.

6. Nothing needs to be changed. All is good just as it is.

7. Welcome every little insecurity or fear you feel.

8. Welcome every aspect of the ego, just as you would embrace a child whom you dearly love.

18 *Inauthenticity in Parenting*

Both trying not to hurt children emotionally and excessively catering to their every need creates inauthentic parenting. An authentic parent wants to serve and love their child, but not to the detriment of themselves. An authentic parent knows that self-love is at the center of the family system, and without it nothing good can truly come into being. As authentic parents, we know that sacrificing ourselves for our children will lead to self-absorbed children. It will also likely pass down to our children the unhealthy ethic of sacrificing oneself for other people. In this model, everyone lives for the future and no one is ever happy.

Being a parent means actively taking care of the next generation. If we truly want the future generations to thrive, we must show them how to live from their hearts in the service of all life by example. The ethic of sacrificing ourselves for the future is neither healthy for ourselves in the now, nor will it teach the future generations a healthy and wholesome way of being. We must serve ourselves what we want and need today, while we hold the future generations in our awareness and actions every day. We know that only through tending to the earth and stewarding her will we have a future. We live for ourselves and future generations while honoring our ancestors. Without them we are nothing.

Story: *The Inauthentic Parent*

I'm going to distill the essence of inauthenticity in parenting through a make-believe story of a particular tendency in parenting. The mother wakes up and the first thing she thinks about is her son. She has no thought for herself—her life is centered around her child. Her son doesn't want the omelet she spent the last 20 minutes making. He wants French toast instead. He's seven and she likes to spoil him by giving him exactly what he wants. She doesn't really feel like cooking another breakfast, but she forces herself to make him French toast. She gets hungry while making it, because it delays her own breakfast and she hasn't gotten her cup of coffee yet.

He is content for 15 minutes before he complains that she hasn't yet bought the new virtual reality headset he was asking for. She feels badly that he's not getting what he wants. He tells her how all his friends have one, and asks when he is going to get his. She remembers how her own parents denied all her little needs and preferences. She never wants him to feel the way she felt as a child.

Does this sound at all familiar? There are many versions of this story about how to lose yourself while parenting. This is just one vignette. If you're a parent, I'm sure you have your own story of losing yourself in your child.

Straight Words: *Parent from Authenticity*

If we want to parent authentically, we need to take care of ourselves first. We don't take care of ourselves in a selfish way, but rather in a way that is centered in self. We need to tend to ourselves and, as they tell us on an airplane, put our own oxygen mask on first. It's not enough to cater to our children's needs in the moment. We also must think about what is best for ourselves in the moment, along with our child's future and the person they are becoming. We raise them to be prepared for their future. We help them to blossom. We look out for the whole field, which includes the parent, child, family, and community. We don't sacrifice ourselves for our children. We find our own will and desires. The most effective parenting is centered on what the parent wants in the service of the whole family.

Game: *Authentic Parenting*

1. Notice all the ways in which you are trying to make yourself a different person so your children will have a better experience.

2. Notice how it feels in your body to try to make yourself a certain way to please them or not hurt them.

3. Stop trying to parent in any way in particular, other than following what your heart wants.

4. Let yourself find your natural way of parenting.

5. Connect with your heart and trust its natural responses.

6. What does your heart feel around your children and your family? What does it notice?

7. Your heart will guide you in how to be an authentic and loving parent.

19 There is No Right Way to Be

Be however you want to be. When you allow yourself to be as you are with no inhibitions or posturing, you return to a natural state. This natural state is effortless and flows from your being outward.

Be like a tree. A tree doesn't try to be right, it just is how it is. I believe trees know there is no right or wrong way to be. When we are as we are, we are naturally how we are meant to be. Adhering to any idea of how we are supposed to be leads us to inauthenticity.

Story: *The Crooked Tree*

There was a pine tree near where I used to live in Ukiah, California that I walked by every day. It grew in a very funny way that was different from all the other trees around it. It did not grow straight. It grew mostly straight, then suddenly turned crooked before straightening out again.

I felt shame arise in me when I looked at the tree. The way it grew crookedly reminded me of where I felt off in myself. But the tree felt no shame—it was as it was. Somehow the shape of the tree showed me where I was out of integrity with myself. The tree's twists and turns showed me where I didn't allow myself to grow as I was meant to naturally grow. I was trying to make the tree of my being grow the way my mind thought it should grow. That seemed to be where the shame was emanating from. This tree had no shame–it just grew how it grew. I love this tree!

Straight Words: *There's No Right or Wrong Way To Be*

There's no right or wrong way to be. You are how you are. You can stop playing the trying game anytime you want. Trying to do the right thing is futile. There's no right thing to be done. There's simply what's true to you and what's in your heart. Honor the truth that you feel and stop trying to be better than you are. The deeper truth comes out when you let go of any idea that you should be different and simply allow yourself to be how you are. The raw and real you have no pretenses and nothing to hide. You are just unadulteratedly you. You are as you are. What could possibly be better?

Game: *Be Like a Tree*

1. Find your favorite local tree.

2. Observe the tree closely and notice how the tree just allows itself to be. The tree knows there's no right or wrong way to be. The tree just is.

3. Imagine the tree as a wise being who has lived here for many years and can give you advice on how to live.

4. Go ahead and ask the tree the questions that are on your heart and mind. Listen with your heart and mind for the reply. Thank the tree for whatever it tells you.

5. Take the tree's perspective and look back at yourself from the tree's vantage point. What do you imagine the tree would sense or perceive about you? How would the tree deal with your problems? What advice does it have?

6. Observe the tree closely again. Open your heart to the tree. Quietly stand or sit with your roots in the soil and let yourself experience what it's like for the world to move around you. You have nowhere to go. You are committed to living in this one spot.

7. Take off your shoes and socks and feel the earth under your bare feet. Let go, allow, and simply imagine your energetic roots going deep into the soil.

8. There's nothing to do, nowhere to go. All you have to do is simply be yourself in this world.

9. Periodically think back on your experience with the tree. Ask yourself: If the tree were in my situation, how would the tree handle it? Thank the tree and take its wisdom into your day.

20 Do What You Want

If the only thing you did in life was be authentic, you would have a good, full, and rich life. The power of authenticity is not fully known on earth. Being authentic is like being Wonder Woman or Superman. It's a profound act of courage which sets us free and makes our heart and soul soar with power and passion to rise in the face of any challenges. It's so true and pure.

Being authentic is a power of the soul to stand true in the face of intense opposition. Being authentic guards you against lies, falsehoods, and evil. You can stay true to yourself and your love in any situation. When you have the power of authenticity firmly on your side, there's no challenge too great for you to meet with your eyes open and head held high. You naturally have faith in yourself and life. You can revel in your courage to remain authentic in the face of all the opposition that exists in our society. So many forces may attempt to hold you down, but your authenticity is impervious to these forces. You become the force of change for a new paradigm by simply being yourself.

Doing what you truly desire and being authentic are intimately connected. Being authentic is simply doing what you feel moved to do from the core of your being.

Story: *Do What You Want*

I woke up this morning and followed the whims and desires of my heart as I do every morning. I watched Venus, Jupiter, Mars, and Saturn ascend in the morning sky before the Sun's rise. I played guitar, and now I'm writing and editing this book. Whenever I want to do something differently, I do it. I stay true to my heart in the moment. When the Sun rises in about an hour, I will watch it rise. As I write, I track the coming of dawn. I look outside and go outside whenever I feel like it. I love the turning of the night into day.

Straight Words: *Simply Be!*

From an authentic place, simply be yourself and do what you want. There's nothing bad that will come of being yourself. If misfortune happens from being yourself, you get to have the comfort of knowing you stayed true to yourself. At the end of the day, all we can really do is stay true to ourselves.

Game: *Do What You Authentically Want*

Initially, play this game when you aren't at work or don't have anything pressing that you "have to" do immediately. Later on, you can extend this game into your whole life.

1. Find some time you can spend on doing this experiment.

2. Notice what you want to do right now out of all the possible actions that are realistic given your environment and set of circumstances.

3. Allow yourself to do exactly what you want. Take the best of what's around or available to you at the moment. Do what inspires you most.

4. As soon as you want to do something else, stop what you are doing and do the new activity.

5. If you are with someone else, allow yourself to say exactly what you want.

6. Notice what happens when you follow exactly what you feel like doing in the moment.

7. If you are unsure of what you want to do, simply sit or stand until an action arises from your being.

SECTION II: Advanced Authenticity

In this section we will address some of the more advanced principles of authenticity. The courage of the heart is a treasure. When we hold the heart as sacred, it can inform all our actions. Let's not let manners, conventions, and social constructs get in our way. The open heart is transformative and loving. The open heart can embrace conflict and confrontations.

Humanity has been held hostage by fear. Authenticity takes a stand for love, as opposed to the unconsciousness that stems from fear. When we stand for authenticity, we stand together with all the great leaders of the past and present who have taken this stand. Rosa Parks, Greta Thunberg, Ralph Waldo Emerson, Frederick Douglass, and so many others stand for authenticity. If you've fallen out of authenticity, it's easy to return again. Real love receives all with open arms; you're always welcome back to the temple of your heart. The heart keeps the door open and the fire stoked, awaiting our return to love.

When I use negative examples of inauthenticity, I consider them cautionary tales to call us back to authenticity. All of my examples of authenticity and inauthenticity are replete with universal truths. I've chosen to draw mostly on examples of everyday inauthenticity from my personal life. We all experience inauthenticity daily within ourselves and in the behavior of others.

Let's take a stand together for authenticity and love. Inauthenticity leads to cruelty and heartlessness. We can learn from each and every encounter. Oftentimes the deeper and more dysfunctional the pattern we encounter, the more we can learn. In this section, the stories I use to illustrate inauthenticity are all examples of what happens when we allow unconscious fear to lead. I always keep the door open for these individuals to return to their hearts, to return to love, and to return to a healthy connection with me again if they ever desire it.

21 True Will is Beyond Trying

In the Star Wars movie, *The Empire Strikes Back*, Yoda says to Luke, "Do or do not, there is no try." When we try, we attempt to force something with our conscious will. Our conscious will can only go so far. Though we can get a job, find a suitable partner, and gain material success, true happiness and deep fulfillment often elude the conscious will. There's another force of will which goes beyond the conscious will. This force is the sentient will. It comes from feeling. It's the force of nature which drives all things. When we tap into this sentient force of nature, we get more in touch with our very human nature. From here, we can allow things to happen. We can be more authentic with ourselves and respectful of who we are.

Story: *Trying*

I have a dear friend who is often stuck in his mind although he is also so pure of heart. Every time I guide him out of his mind, he tries to follow me by using his mind. The more he tries consciously, the farther he gets from his feelings. If you can pardon my pun, the whole thing is a very trying process. I feel like I'm Yoda and he is Luke.[11] I'm encouraging my friend to be who he is naturally without his mind interfering. Yet, he keeps taking his mind and using it to usurp any of the principles I'm showing him. He has been so deeply identified with his mind that sometimes he thinks his mind is who he is.

After working with him for several years, I can see that he was pretending to want to grow. He didn't really want to walk this way of the heart. The trying was a form of pretending so I would accept him and work with him. Now that he stopped pretending, the dynamic feels more authentic. We are no longer working together, which feels right. He is still on his journey of finding the truth. Sometimes this journey is circuitous. Sometimes we need to live in lies until we can find and face the truth. I honor the way everyone must walk. And I resolutely stand against his inauthenticity. When he finds his authenticity again, he will find a lifelong friend in me.

When I realized how much he was deceiving me, I returned to the truth of my heart. By facing the truth of his deception as well as the deceptions of several other people, I found the safety of my open

---

[11] Characters from the *Star Wars* movie franchise. Yoda is Luke's mentor.

heart again. The sentient will is intuitive and moves with the flow of synchronicity.

Straight Words: *End Trying*

Trying is inauthentic! By trying, we aren't trusting our nature, so we use effort to try to be different than we are. Original sin is a huge lie which haunts humanity. The belief that there's something wrong with our nature plagues us and makes us work against ourselves. This idea divides us from ourselves and puts us in an endless trying game. If we believe there's something wrong with us, we must do our best to be different and overcome our nature. When we fight against our nature, we will be forever stuck in trying.

We are all born with nearly limitless potential. We have both the potential to be innocent and pure, and the potential to be evil and manipulative. If we're born innocent and we don't need to try and make ourselves better, then why does evil exist? The question as to why evil exists has plagued philosophers and theologians alike.

Evil has a particular role in authenticity. Evil helps us to learn to be who we are in the face of inauthenticity. Why do movies and video games have villains? We can use trials and tribulations to hone our skills, but we must not begin to believe our nature is evil. When we believe our nature is evil, we have to control ourselves with our conscious will if we wish to act or be good. This control is a reaction to the deeply unconscious belief that we are inherently bad. When our actions are motivated by fear, they draw us towards evil.

We live in a deeply wounded world, and many of us need help to heal from the wounds we carry in our hearts and bodies. Unconscious fear comes from unprocessed trauma. Unconscious fear opens the door to evil and invites it in. All people who engage in rape, murder, molestation, and discrimination are unconsciously coming from trauma.

In order to have true freedom, we must have the freedom to go against our nature. When we go against our nature in a way that contains cruelty, there is a state of imbalance that we can call evil. It's not a permanent state of affairs. It's simply something that is out of balance and needs help returning to the love of the tribe. When we return to our natural state, evil is dispelled. By allowing ourselves to be ourselves, the goodness that is within us blazes forth. If someone is deeply lost in trauma, it may take a long time to open their heart. It's always good to follow our own heart and choose who we want to relate with at this time.

Game: *The End of Trying*

1. Reflect on a time when you were trying so hard to make something happen. Even though your perseverance may have been admirable, notice how ineffective and unnecessary the trying was.

2. Since we are meant to enjoy life, set a strong intention to have as much fun as possible. Imagine doing the same thing you did in the past with more ease and play.

3. Play with ending all trying in your heart. Make a strong commitment or playful vow with yourself.

4. Whenever you catch yourself trying throughout the day, simply stop and allow. When we allow ourselves to be as we are, we don't try to stop ourselves from trying. Any attempt to not try will put you back in the trying game.

5. Simply let yourself be and you will naturally end all trying. If trying should arise again, simply allow it to arise.

6. Notice the true will that is underneath all the trying.

7. Get in touch with your deeper will as it moves you.

8. Live from your will and love it.

22 Be Free From Societal Constraints

We can only be truly free when we free ourselves from the tyranny of society and the tortured voices that tell us what we should do. When the voice of "should" no longer corrupts our minds, we have our full freedom to think, feel, and do whatever we want, without any force oppressing or opposing us.

Story: *The Man Who Moved Against Society*

Nelson Mandela was born in South Africa. In 1948, the South African government adopted apartheid– one of the most horrific and systematic forms of racism that has existed on this earth. Mandela did not accept the unjust laws of society. He and many others resisted the corruption. He fought in the courts, roused the people to organize in the streets, and weathered years of unjust imprisonment on Robben Island. There were many others who fought in this struggle alongside Mandela.

Racism is still a widespread problem in this world. Mandela took a stand against the grave injustice in South African society. This helped South Africa eventually overthrow the apartheid regime. We must follow in his footsteps–it's up to all of us to take our stand against the injustices in our world today.

Straight Words: *Stand for Truth*

We must not blindly follow the sins of society. Some laws favor the rich and discriminate against the poor. Some laws favor the tan skinned people we call white and discriminate against all shades of the brown-skinned people we call black, yellow, and red (all non-"whites"). Gender discrimination has become the new racism. Transgender people are often not recognized as the gender they identify with. Some people say that biology and gender are one and the same, so therefore gender is not a choice. This perspective both lacks empathy for transgender individuals and doesn't understand the social constructs behind gender. Authenticity has the power to end all forms of discrimination.

Take a stand for what you believe in, even when it's contrary to what's accepted in society. In many ways, modern society is full of lies. Much of our society runs on fear. In most countries, the political system is deeply broken. There's almost no one representing integrity. Or if they are, they typically get nowhere in the current political system. When society is so far from the heart, it needs to bend its knees and bow to the way of the heart. We must always serve the integrity of the heart.

Game: *Dance with the Tyranny of Society*

1. Notice the big bad society that's been imposing all its rules on you. Imagine it as a large villain bearing down on you.

2. In what way(s) is this villain constraining your behavior?

3. List each constraint one by one in your mind.

4. Notice where you feel pressured to be a certain way to fit in or belong. Notice where you feel a lack of freedom.

5. Just breathe that pressure out on the exhale. Breathe in acceptance for yourself just as you are as you inhale.

6. Imagine you are larger than a star. As a star, the big bad villain of society is tiny and you cannot fit into it. Let society fit into you. Let both this villain and the whole of society be a part of your grand and outrageously unfolding hero's journey.

7. You are vast. You contain the infinite.

8. Even though you don't like the societal conditioning which exists, notice all the ways it is helping you to grow. It may be teaching

you patience, perseverance, or any number of other lessons.

9. Allow yourself to be the person who is capable of making a difference. When you believe in yourself and your capacities, and do what you are moved to, you can make a tremendous impact in this world. This impact measures beyond any way our minds can conceive of.

10. Come into acceptance of it all as it is right now. Accept your feelings of outrage and accept the way society is.

11. Dance with societal conditioning. Do what you feel moved in your heart to do in response to it.

12. Stay in your heart and remember your vastness. Take any action you choose to take from your open heart.

23 Open the Door to the Miraculous

When we surrender to our deeper being, we enter the realm of the miraculous. Who we are is so full and replete with power and impact that our unique gifts blaze forth and we become like a star. We shine. We don't ask permission, we simply shine in the way we are meant to. We become a beacon lighting up the world around us and lighting the way for future generations. When we shine, we change everything around us just like a shining star changes the night sky.

Story: *Miraculous Authenticity*

When my father was on his deathbed, he had been in a coma for 14 days from a blood clot that temporarily stopped his heart. My girlfriend at the time, Heather, my Uncle Shiraz, and I all sat around my father as he entered the last stages of the dying process. He was as he always had been—authentic. The dying process is often a hyper authentic state. Anything that's being hidden just comes out and there's really nothing to hide anymore.

He sort of glanced at each one of us, his eyes slightly tearing-up with gratitude each time. It was miraculous. Even through the coma, he communicated his love so clearly and deeply that

Heather and I both had the same experience. We witnessed a gratitude ceremony which started with me on his left, moving to Heather in the middle, and ending with Shiraz on his right. He had so much love and appreciation coming through him that being with him in his last moments of life on earth opened my heart. I feel as if this experience made me a wiser person and opened me up to realms of being I had not known before.

Straight Words: *Authenticity is a Miracle*

Authenticity is the essence of life. Nature is authentic. She doesn't waste time with politeness. The sun doesn't ask for permission to rise. The stars don't seek approval for shining their light. Things are as they are. When we return to our nature, we realize we are miracles.

Game: *Open to Everyday Miracles*

1. Play make-believe like you are a child. Only this make-believe game is more real than reality.

2. Close your eyes. Remember the miraculous is all around you.

3. Now open your eyes. Notice what's around you and what's in you. Look at the miracle of this amazing creation before you.

4. This is your great art. This is what you have
    manifested in this life. Notice you are alive.
    What are the odds of that?

5. Notice all the forces that had to conspire
    together biologically, genealogically,
    geologically, astronomically, spiritually, and
    existentially to make your existence possible.

6. Notice all the evolutionary forces of love.
    Give a nod to all the ancestors who had to be
    paired in just the right way to produce you.
    Feel into the whole existence of life having to
    be this way so that you could be alive on earth
    now.

7. Notice the fact that you've gotten this far
    without dying or killing yourself. You've come
    through all the trials you've experienced to be
    here at this moment reading this book. If
    you're anything like me, that's a miracle in and
    of itself.

8. Open your heart in gratitude to all the little
    and big miracles which are around you every
    day—loved ones, pets, friends, all the beautiful
    nature around you and the stars above you,
    the planets, the moon, and the sun.

9. And remember the greatest miracle of all—you!

24 We Are Part of Nature

As much as many humans like to pretend we are somehow separate or greater than nature, we are a part of nature. Our bodies are bound to the same cycles that all natural creatures are. We are born. We live for a short time and then we die. In many ways, we are really not that different from any other species on the planet. We live and make the best of our surroundings to serve ourselves and our lives.

We are capable of a quality of self-awareness which few other species seem to possess. This awareness helps us to modify our environment in a way that perhaps only beavers come close to doing. Beavers are the only other animals who dramatically change their habitat by the way they build dams in a river. However, when we modify our surroundings in a way that threatens the environment for ourselves and others, we step out of the natural order of things. When we pollute the earth and take resources without considering consequences, we become destructive. If we use our self-awareness capacities for good, we will become stewards of nature who look out for the best interests of all life.

Authenticity

Story: *Human Nature*

I used to be ashamed of my sexuality. I used to feel like it was somehow wrong. Now I treat my sexuality as part of my nature, like I treat my hunger and thirst. When I'm horny, I touch myself. Just as when I'm hungry, I eat, and when I'm thirsty, I drink. I honor the sexual impulse as a part of human nature. I love and enjoy my sexuality. When someone I'm with wants to explore with me who I also want to explore with sexually, I honor this as well.

Straight Words: *We Are Nature*

The separation between humans and the rest of nature needs to stop. It's not right to pretend that humans are special and different from every other living thing on earth. We are a part of nature. It's because we see ourselves as separate that we often treat nature as an object to be used. Nature is a part of you and she needs to be cherished. When we stop treating nature as an object, we realize we are nature. We are human beings, a species on planet Earth, who are connected to all other life forms. Every species is unique. Every species is special. And each and every species is an essential part of the great web of life.

Game: *Human Nature*

1. Go to your favorite spot in nature. Any spot with trees, the ocean, a desert, mountains, rivers, lakes, or another aspect of nature will do fine.

2. Look out at the scene and admire it. Notice the features of the landscape you are in. It may contain trees, birds, bushes, mountains, or other wildlife.

3. Admire all that you see and extend your gratitude to it. Bless everything around you.

4. Now look inside yourself to your own nature.

5. Notice that your nature is like the nature around you. This is your human nature.

6. You can know your human nature through feeling it. It's just like feeling your heart and your intuition.

7. Open to your human nature as if you're an inner landscape, seascape, or skyscape.

8. Admire your vastness and wildness. Dance into the mystery of the undiscovered worlds inside your nature.

9. Embrace your whole nature just as it is—the good and the bad, the beautiful and the ugly. Accept all of who you truly are.

25 Politeness vs. Authenticity

Kindness is good. The golden rule is wonderful. Treating others how we want to be treated is essential to creating a world that works for everyone. However, politeness is like putting on excessive manners instead of just being authentic. When truth is what is called for, let's be honest. Saying what you really feel is never wrong. Of course it is ideal to speak the truth with kindness. Treating other people in a way that nurtures connection and engenders love is never a bad thing. However, excessive politeness and inauthentic niceness compromise authenticity. When we open to the love in our heart, we naturally act in a loving way toward all our relations.

Story: *Authenticity Trumps Politeness*

When my Aunt started unduly influencing my grandmother to cut my mother out of the will, my parents got wind of what was happening. My father confronted my aunt directly about her lies and deception. He told her exactly how he felt about what she was doing. He was righteously angry. There was no reason to disinherit my mother. It only drove an unnecessary wedge through our family. My aunt said that he was being rude and hostile to her. Yet, it was she who was being passive aggressive and hostile. She had lied, manipulated, and stolen what rightfully belonged to my mother. My father was being unfairly cast as the villain. He was simply being authentic and true. I always admired him for having the courage to speak his mind, even when it was not polite and it made things difficult. Thank you, Dad! I miss you so much. There's not a day that goes by that my thoughts don't reach out and touch you.

Straight Words: *Always Be Real*

The conditioning to be polite over being real is based on a fear of our fundamental nature. When you believe your nature is bad, you must be taught to be polite. Children are real. They say what they feel. Teaching children to be kind and considerate of others is good. Children can be selfish and not think of others. They need to be guided to be loving and connected. However, teaching children to be polite versus being real can be disrespectful to their being. When we force children to be nice, we may inadvertently train them to be inauthentic.

It's good to follow what's in our heart as the guide for what to do. The heart is never wrong. Yet it will sometimes go against certain manners. When I look at the way I expressed my love for my father in the story before this section, it doesn't seem completely appropriate to the flow of the writing. While it breaks with the convention, it is truly authentic to what my heart is saying.

I believe that if we embody more unconventional authenticity in little ways, we will be *more* free. Let's all feel love for the ones we love. We can express this love however we are moved to. Don't wait for it to be okay or acceptable. Express as you feel moved to. It's good to take the other person or people you are with into consideration as you express yourself. And we don't need to be polite. It's okay to be who we truly are.

Game: *Tickle the Tyranny of the Polite*

1. Find someone who can handle directness and authenticity.

2. Notice when you are with them and you feel the urge to be polite.

3. Experiment with being slightly rude in the service of authenticity. This "rudeness" is not meant to be mean. It's simply being direct in a way some people may interpret as offensive.

4. Say something authentic which may be a bit edgy. Do this with just enough humor or levity to make the medicine go down. The

humor is meant to ease the directness and help the other person receive the truth.

5. Notice how it feels to let yourself be even a little more authentic than usual.

6. Flirt with the edge of what is acceptable and notice what happens when you are both direct and lighthearted.

26 Authenticity is Natural

Authenticity is natural, just like a bird, a deer, or a flower. There's a natural way to be that is the way we are meant to be. Identification with fear makes us inauthentic. When we are ruled by fear, we never find who we truly are meant to be. Fear is here to help us develop courage. We must use our fear to courageously enhance our lives, not to make us smaller. It's okay to have fear. It's even okay to act from it. As soon as you notice fear is present, stop acting from fear and return to your authentic self. The easiest way to do this is to come into loving acceptance of the fear. When we embrace our fears with love, we naturally become authentic.

Story: *A Natural Leader*

Samantha has been training with me to lead my company, Bridging Worlds Behavioral Services. I did not offer her the position because of her experience as an executive director. Instead, I offered her the position because of her purity of heart and authenticity. She is the right person for the job. While it's very hard to teach someone to have purity of heart, it's much easier to teach someone the basics of leadership. At first she tried to pretend that she knew how to be an executive director better than she did. She may have been afraid that if I really knew how bad she was with certain aspects of the job, she might lose the position. She tried to cover up what she didn't know by handling certain situations the way she thought I would handle them.

When she acts naturally as herself, she is the best leader she can possibly be. If she tries to be like me or do what she thinks I want, she becomes inauthentic. When we are first learning a new job, the conditioning is to cover up what we don't know. Samantha had been acting out this pattern during the early days of taking on her new position. As I showed her how to simply be authentic with what she didn't know how to do, we were both relieved. Since then, she has been able to come to me more transparently with the obstacles she faces. It's so much easier. She's also learning that she has her own style of leadership. To come into herself as a leader, she has to do things differently than how I would do them. It's wonderful to witness and participate in her blossoming leadership. She is truly a natural leader.

Straight Words: *Authenticity Is Natural*

It's not so terrifying to be yourself. In fact, it's scarier to not be yourself. There's only one thing you are meant to do and that's be yourself. It's never too late to be authentic. Many people are inauthentic through much of their life. It's hard to be inauthentic at death. As people come closer to death they often come closer to the authenticity of their heart.

Game: *Letting Go of Fear*

1. Notice what is occupying your mind. Our thoughts often turn to the things we are afraid of.

2. Feel the fear you feel underneath whatever you've been thinking about.

3. Find where you feel the fear in your body. Notice how the energy feels. Is it tight or loose? Hard or soft? Moving or still? Warm or cool? Light or heavy?

4. Hold tight to the fear and let it control you for a moment.

5. Notice how this feels in your body.

6. Now embrace the energy associated with this fear. Allow yourself to feel it more fully with loving acceptance.

7. As you embrace the energy with acceptance, notice your relationship to the fear. It's no longer running you.

8. As you breathe out, let go of any residual
    attachment to fear so you are no longer run
    by it. Simply let the breath help you find the
    right relationship with this energy.

9. As you breathe, continue to let go of your
    identity attachment to the fear and allow
    yourself to be as you naturally are.

10. Notice how it feels to be free of fear. You are
    the one who feels all the feelings, but as you
    realize you are not the feelings you will be set
    free. You are the lover and all feelings are
    your beloved. True emotional freedom comes
    in loving all that you feel right now.

27 Clarity in Contemplating Death

The power of love transcends time and space. Death does not erase anything. Every action you've ever done stays in the flow of eternity even though your body will turn to dust. Everything that you have built will be torn down like sandcastles crumbling before the relentless seas of time. One day you will be completely forgotten by the living. Yet your actions still matter. They become part of the swirl that is existence. In the end, it's only the love that matters. Nothing else remains. When you know you are going to die, this truth brings life into focus. The presence of death brings us into an authentic relationship with life.

Story: *Harnessing the Power of Death*

For eighteen years I was in a mind control cult run by an abusive and narcissistic leader. While I was in the cult, I believed there was a chance I could live forever if I loved and accepted all my feelings. I didn't immediately adopt this belief, but rather it was instilled in me over time. I increasingly experienced the amazing benefits of loving my feelings, and my life began to transform. Learning to love my feelings gave me incredible skills and capacities that I base my life's work around. There was so much truth in this approach.

Many spiritual paths have sought physical immortality. And there are stories from many traditions about people who have lived for hundreds of years. The leader had lost his younger sister at an early age. This loss sent his mother into a mental institution. Instead of grieving this loss fully and coming to terms with it, he created a false persona centered around denying the impact of this loss. He believed that he would find a way to alter the very fabric of the universe. He created a fantasy of grandeur instead of feeling the fragility and hardness of his loss. I believe this was a way to avoid the fear and pain he felt at the loss of his sister. It seems he did this to avoid going temporarily insane as his mother did. I hadn't realized how much his fantasy around ending the process of death for all humanity came from trauma. He was seeking physical immortality in this body. The deeper I got into the group, the more I trusted his authority.

I thought that if he believed it, it must be true. He was so reliable, helpful, and consistent in so many ways. I've always been open to unusual ideas. Even after this experience, I still keep an open mind. However, I'm more careful about vetting people and ideas. I had adopted his dream and I was working to get out of this cycle of birth and death.

I had thought that the very fabric of the universe was based on traumas that we could reverse.

As I got more honest with myself and my heart, I realized I wanted to live my life fully and then die. I'm so grateful for the impermanence of this life's existence. Even if I could live forever, I know I wouldn't want to. I started imagining exactly how I want to die, if it happens as I choose.

As I imagined my death, my whole life came into focus. I understand more clearly my mission in being here and founded the nonprofit Heart-Centered Revolutions. Deep in my heart, I found a desire that I believe is inside of everyone's heart. We all want a world that works for everyone. Each of us can become seeds of the revolution by connecting to our hearts. One day I believe this idea will spread far and wide. I hope that it will help us to have more empathy and love in the world for each other.

This book along with an entire body of work came into focus as I contemplated my death. I knew what I had to do before I died, so I started putting things in order for my final days. Every action I've done and will continue to do embraces the impermanence of life. I live my life honoring the inevitable approach of death. I love my death and await our meeting at the appointed time and place.

When I am done with my life's work, I intend to keep my date with destiny and dance with death. I want to live fully and first do what I came here to do so I can die when I'm done.

My hope is that when my day comes, I will know I laid it all on the playing field and held nothing back. If the universe allows it, I want to complete my life's work. Once I'm done, I will welcome death with open arms. I see death as governed by the Norns of Norse mythology, who are female beings that create and control fate. These three sisters of fate weave the strands of our life. I honor them and my fate. I do not wish to transcend my fate but only to face it, feel it, and live life as fully as I possibly can.

Straight Words: *Hold Nothing Back*

You are going to die. The form in which you currently live will one day give out. What do you want to do while you're alive? Now is the time to live. Live with death over your shoulder. Imagine your death could happen at any time. Hold nothing back from life. Love the people you love and live your life fully, as if you or they could die at any moment.

Game: *Imagining Death*

1. Imagine your death.

2. Think about the ways you would most likely
    die.

    a. You could die of natural causes when
        the body says it's time.

    b. You could die in an accident, such as a
        car or plane crash.

    c. Someone else could end your life by
        murder or manslaughter.

    d. You could die by suicide if you chose
        to take your own life.

3. As you feel into these possibilities, notice how
    you feel about each one. Which one do you
    feel more of an affinity for? Which one do
    you feel more of an aversion to? Simply notice
    and allow.

4. What if you were to die right now? How
    would you feel? What would be incomplete in
    your life? What would you most wish you had
    done?

5. Notice that this is what you are still alive on
    earth to complete.

6. Pray to death itself to help you complete your life. For example, "Death, please help me accomplish what I'm here to do." Even if you don't relate to death as an entity, imagining it this way gives you a way to relate with this force or presence. If this feels right, experiment with it and see what happens. You can also pray to whatever other force you prefer if that resonates more.

7. Sit in meditation as deeply as you need to in order to feel your life's purpose. What are you here to do? Feel for it and let a vision come into being. You'll know it's right because it will feel expansive and inspiring. (If you have trouble finding this it may not be the right time or you may want to seek assistance.)

8. Live fully each day. The best way to get your affairs in order is to embody your aliveness now. Begin tending to your life's mission, and all you want to tend to in life, as if you might die at any time.

9. Notice all the ways in which you already are completing your life's purpose naturally. Be sure to get as far as you truly want to get in completing your life's mission every day.

10. Remember to enjoy it all, relax, and have fun. Death and life don't need to be too serious. When we laugh with the great mysteries of the universe, we embody the joy we were meant to embody in both life and in death.

28 Your Superpower

When you achieve a level of mastery with authenticity, you no longer have to over think your actions in order to determine the best course. You can feel and let the actions channel from the core of your being. This is a superpower because it ends a lot of the needless cycles of stress and trying which we've all been trapped in. Instead of managing what you are going to say in your mind, let the words flow out from your heart and soul.

Story: *Authentic Superhero*

Hector was a person who came to speak at my high school in 1994. He was someone who had a lot of success in college and partied very hard. He had a drunken fall from a window that permanently paralyzed him. Hector had a lot of self-acceptance around his story and experience. He made a new career for himself as a motivational speaker through sharing his tale of tragedy. He was on his way to being a professional athlete when everything was stripped from him. There had been warning signs, like partying too much and blacking out, but he ignored them. His story stayed with me and helped me realize that I didn't want to drink my way through college. I wanted to have fun in other ways. Hector was an authentic superhero. He overcame huge adversity and continues to inspire my life now, along with all of the other lives he touched.

Straight Words: *Honesty is Precious*

Honesty is so rare that when you have the power to speak the truth, you become a light to all those around you. You become a literal superhero of your world. Be authentic. Be true. Be heroic. Be yourself. No one else can do it for you. Only you can claim the throne of who you truly are.

Game: *Unveil Your Superhero Nature*

1. When you are wholly yourself, notice you have a superpower.

2. If you were a superhero with your power, what would it be? (My superpower is the ability to feel everything inside of myself and others.)

3. What's your superpower? Just take a gift you already have and exaggerate it to epic proportions. (For example, I will lead the whole world in an empathy and love revolution.)

4. Take your time and really feel it from your heart. What are you here to do? What do you do best?

5. Enjoy your superpower. It may be dormant. If you notice it, let it shine with your loving attention. It will develop over time as you are yourself. All superpowers do.

29 The Layers of Truth

There is always a deeper layer of truth underneath the one you are living from now. When you are committed to authenticity, you are committed to truth. When the truth is spoken, you will be open to it. Even if it's difficult to hear, you will be able to hear it. We would rather be open to the truth than cling to some false sense of ego-driven identity.

Story: *Layered Authenticity*

I started noticing a pattern in my friend David. Sometimes he would hide some of the layers of feeling around his romantic relationship. I guided him to imagine that his entire being was a 20-layer cake of awareness. He didn't fully understand where I was coming from and balked at my suggestion. So I guided him to start at the second or third layer down before dropping down to about layer nine or ten. As he dropped deeper into his being, he began to feel the fear that was underneath his relationship pattern.

After that, everything changed. He had a peak experience as he dropped to a much deeper layer of himself than he had previously experienced. He still goes in and out of deeper layers as we all do.

Dropping into a deeper layer allowed him to experience the fullness of his being. This experience seemed to help him get to the core of what was going on underneath and let go of some of the jealousy that was impacting his relationship.

Straight Words: *Honesty Comes From Depth*

True honesty comes from the deeper layers of our being. When we are at the surface layer, our honesty may only be as deep as we are aware of at the moment. We often don't know ourselves well if at all in our deeper layers. This can result in having an element of dishonesty underneath. By connecting with our deepest feelings possible, we maximize our authenticity.

Game: *Dropping to Deeper Layers*

1. Imagine there's always a deeper layer to wherever you are currently feeling.

2. Notice what layer you feel yourself to be at right now on a scale of 1-20. If you're reading and thinking, it's unlikely that you are higher than 5 unless you are having a peak experience. If you are identified in your mind, then you are at layers 1-3. In our normal state of awareness, we are generally 1-3 layers down. If you are a particularly aware person,

you may begin at layers 3-6. Wherever you start, unless you are in a profoundly peak experience right now, you probably aren't beyond layer 10.

3. Imagine that the thought you're having right now is on the surface and feel for what's underneath this thought. Notice what is there. What do you experience below the surface of the thought?

4. Intend to go to a deeper level of awareness. Use your feelings to feel for what is underneath and simply drop your awareness to a deeper level.

5. You'll know you've arrived at a deeper layer when you feel more connected to yourself and your feelings.

6. Let go of any ideas you have about who you think you are and come into what you really feel at this moment.

7. Slow down. Touch your heart with your hand.

8. Notice what you *really* feel.

9. Continue dropping layers by feeling into the center of what you are experiencing and going to what is just underneath.

10. As you drop to a deeper layer, notice how your awareness shifts outside of your mind. You can feel more of yourself from here. Everything is a little different. Colors may be brighter, sounds may seem altered, things may appear slower.

11. It's good to fluidly shift layers at any time as the needs of your life change. Deeper is not always better. For greater freedom, choose the layer you want to be at in the moment.

12. As you move through your day, track what layer you are at. Drop to a deeper layer as you feel moved by simply feeling your feelings more fully and allowing them to be present.

30 It's Okay to be Afraid

Being authentic about our fear is a wonderful way to loosen its grip on us. Having fear is not a problem. Being run by fear is a different story. When we suppress or pretend we don't have fears, we empower them to run our lives. When we face our fears honestly, admit to them, and do not let them stop us from being outrageously ourselves, then we can open to life, love, and authentic living.

Story: *The Embrace of Fear*

I began to pursue my passion for acting in college. I loved acting, but I was terrified to get up on stage in front of other people and perform. I remember my first big performance. I got so nervous and scared, I didn't know how I was going to do it. My teacher had given me a tip to embrace my fear and use it for the performance. I remember opening fully to the energy within my fear and using it to act from. When I embraced this powerful energy and harnessed it, I had so much presence in my acting.

Nowadays, when I'm scared of something, like teaching a new group, I simply either say my fear out loud or admit it to myself. Once I know I'm scared, the fear no longer has any power over me.

I embrace the energy of the fear and go to my edge. I love walking on the edge and adventuring on the wild side. As soon as I'm able to feel and open to my fear, it loses its hold over me and I become a channel of love.

Straight Words: *How to Deal With Fear*

Fear is not a problem when we are direct and honest. When we can say "this scares me," fear loses its hold over us. Be honest with fear. Be fearless. If you don't mind a little crassness, take it by the balls and don't let it run your life. You are in charge. By being the lover of this fear, you truly take your power back.

Game: *Love Fear*

1. Notice where you are holding some fear in your body.

2. Simply breathe into that area and notice how it feels. Is it tight or loose? Moving or still? Hard or soft? Sharp or dull?

3. Allow the fear to be here in your body. Now, let go.

4. Don't try to control your actions, and don't try to get rid of the fear.

5. Just allow it to be here as it is. When you accept the fear, it has no hold over you.

6. Allow the fear to exist without clinging to it. Embrace it, love it, and let it be inside of you.

7. The energy inside of fear is a very valuable resource. By accepting the fear, you can now harness this energy and use it in any way you want.

31 The Greatest Art

Your life is the greatest work of art imaginable. It has all the elements necessary for you to learn, grow, and evolve in just the way that is right for you. You are manifesting this grand work in every moment. Enjoy, rejoice, and bask in it.

Story: *Manifesting Arts*

When I lived in Ukiah, I used to go on a walk. Whenever I crossed this one gate, I said to myself, "Everything on the other side of this fence is a portal into my great soul's mystery." As soon as I walked through the gate, the crows and trees would call to me and tell me things about myself, my history, and my destiny. It was here that I encountered the crooked tree mentioned in an earlier chapter.

I used these walks to help me manifest the next layers of my journey and unfold myself. Each walk brought me back pieces of my unconscious so I could remember who I am and my purpose in being here. The perspectives that came forward on these walks have stayed with me and deepened over time.

Straight Words: *You Are a Masterpiece*

What if you were the masterpiece of a great artist? Stop looking at yourself as some flawed, messed up thing, and look at yourself through the lens of love. You are one of the greatest masterpieces to have ever come into existence. Honor that every other person is a masterpiece as well. You're no better or worse than anyone or anything else.

Game: *Open to the Masterpiece*

1. Imagine your life as the greatest work of art ever created.

2. See yourself as the hero of this artful masterpiece.

3. Now remember an experience of adversity you went through during an earlier time in life, perhaps in childhood or adolescence. Feel into the emotions and overall mood of this adversity.

4. Notice and appreciate how this adversity has shaped your character and made you into who you are today.

5. Now, think of and notice a recent adversity you've gone through.

6. Open your heart to this adversity. It will continue to shape your character and help make you into an even better person as you open your heart to its challenges.

7. Feel it all! Breathe it in and let yourself feel even the most painful feelings around this adversity.

8. Embrace everything that's brought you here. Embrace the good and the bad. Embrace the beautiful and the ugly. Welcome it all!

9. Notice that right here inside of you are all the creative elements needed to have your dreams come true.

10. Thank your beautiful, authentic heart for carrying you through so much.

11. Embrace the masterpiece that is your life.

12. Embrace the great artist behind the masterpiece of your life. You might call this your deeper being, God, the Universe, or a combination of all of them.

13. Be grateful to all the unseen forces that support this great masterpiece of life. Open your heart in gratitude to all our wondrous relations.

32 Compliments

When I tell someone something I admire about them, they often thank me. I will sometimes let them know that I didn't mean it as a compliment. I was simply stating the truth, and there is no need for thanks. If the truth was something that appeared to be more negative, then I would say that. When we are authentic, we do not gear things toward compliments—we simply say what is true.

It's good to notice what people do well and appreciate it. It's good to notice what people do poorly and correct it. Both are an act of love. When you do them both from empathy, neither one is more or less loving than the other. Often, praise feels better to receive than correction. (Additionally, giving praise often feels better than giving corrections.) That's only because we are typically identified with our ego. When we are connected to our deeper being, receiving (and giving) authentic correction feels better than courteous praise.

Story: *Non-Complimentary*

I remember telling Steve, my administrative director, how well he was doing at a task. He thanked me for the compliment. I told him I didn't mean it as a compliment, I meant it as a statement of fact. I said, "If you were doing a shitty job, I would have told you that as well." He appreciates this about me and I treasure the kind of directness we can have with each other. This is the way I hold compliments and appreciation. I'm just sharing the facts of my experience. Oftentimes people take compliments as a stroke to their ego. I mean them as an acknowledgement and recognition of their being underneath. When we don't take compliments and insults personally, we can see the accuracy in what they are pointing toward.

Straight Words: *Take Honest Truth Over Compliments*

Let's end the practice of falsely complimenting each other and just tell each other the truth. A lot of the truth will seem complimentary because when we are in our hearts, we have a lot of good to say about each other. Oftentimes, compliments are used as manipulative ploys to get people to do something or like you. If you're simply being authentic, there's no need for compliments or coercion. We simply want what is best for everyone.

Game: *Anti-Complimenting*

1. Find a friend or someone who is willing to receive radical honesty.

2. Practice telling them the honest truth. Find a few examples of what could seem like compliments. Now, deliver them in such a way that you are just stating a basic fact.

3. No excessiveness or false flattery is needed. For example, "The work you did on that project was thorough and attentive. I really appreciate it. It made my work a whole lot easier."

4. Now deliver a statement which might seem negative. Something like, "When you were talking just now, it seemed to me that you were avoiding yourself and pretending to be alright." (Whatever you say needs to be true to your experience in the moment.)

5. Deliver both kinds of statements in a neutral tone of voice as if you're giving driving directions.

6. Notice how it feels for both of you to be this honest and direct with each other.

33 *Authenticity in the Workplace*

Work culture is often ruled by complete inauthenticity. We've all heard these ridiculous directives:

> "Leave your personal life at the door."
> "Please your boss at all costs."
> "Do it right and don't make any mistakes."

When we believe these restrictive thought forms, they will torture us at work every day. We are conditioned to sell our time to our employer, and they are conditioned to dictate what we do. This is not freedom; this is indentured servitude. No one can or should ever own your time. A free human being is not beholden to anyone else—not their boss, partner, spouse, or child. If authenticity is what we seek, we must be truly free.

How can this work? When people find their right job, they enjoy their work. Because they enjoy their work, it's no longer slavery. It's a choice. We want to do good work and take pride in what we do. As long as the employer is not exploiting the worker and the worker enjoys their job and the company, we are in a free system. The employer and employee enter into an agreement which either one can change. This is ideal for freedom. A good employer will never fire a worker unless they compromise the values of the company or are working against the interests of the whole. A good employee will only leave the company when it's no longer the right fit for them. Ideally each one gives the other ample notice when separation comes.

Story: *An Authentic Workplace*

I founded Bridging Worlds Behavioral Services in 2012 to support developmentally disabled youth and adults. We've always employed excellent people who work well with our clients. However, some of them struggled to relate with their colleagues in the work environment. They weren't accustomed to using empathy and compassion, and they judged me for my candor and honesty.

From reading this book, you might notice that I'm a fairly intense, direct, and honest person. I write this book in a similar tone to how I lead my company. Some of the employees wanted me to act like the more traditional boss they had grown to expect. Essentially, they wanted me to be a different person than I am. I was caught in a codependent relationship as I tried to change myself to meet their expectations. Once I realized that I needed to surround myself with loving and empathic people, I stopped putting up with the unreasonable demands coming from some of the staff. I started calling people out when they lacked empathy. In the phase of life I was in at that time, I raised my voice, cursed, and took a strong stand for the values of the company.

Many of the staff ended up leaving because they couldn't handle the intensity and honesty. They said my authenticity was unloving and toxic. While an element of reactivity was present as a result of my PTSD from being in a narcissistic cult, I do not believe I was ever unloving. I had their best interests at heart even when I was yelling. It was the most loving thing I could do at the time. I was acknowledging the ways in which they were shutting down both their and my potential. I believe my authenticity contributed to their journey in finding the right place for themselves as they moved on from the company. After some time and many changes, we now have a beautifully authentic work culture with people who support and have each other's backs.

Straight Words: *Be Authentic at Work*

If you run a business, make your work environment a place where people can be themselves. If you work for someone else, find a place which allows you the freedom to be yourself.

We should not tolerate jobs that enslave us, or employers who don't look out for our best interests.

Game: *Make Your Work Fun*

1. Take whatever job you have and make it fun.

2. Simply act as if you're playing a game which makes the job fun.

3. For example, you could be going undercover as a spy pretending to be a desk clerk or a grocer. You could be playing an enlightenment game through being a factory worker. You could be waiting tables and practicing the study of human behavior while becoming an expert in psychology and social dynamics. If you work with clients as a therapist or coach, pretend the client is bringing you your next lesson.

4. Every time you do the task, act as if it is a spiritual practice bringing you closer to God or the Universe.

5. Imagine that your teacher is the next person who comes into your world.

6. Imagine the next piece of work that you do is the next part of fulfilling your destiny here on Earth.

7. Take whatever job you have and spice it up with your own genuine interests in a way that honors you.

8. Observe how your work changes when you play with it.

34 Imprisoning Relationships

Inauthenticity can rule our primary relationships. When you imprison a partner with your expectations, you trap them in one way of relating. This binds both you and them into playing a petty game in an unconscious torture chamber where neither one of you can have what you really want.

A truly loving relationship is one where you set each other free to be yourselves. You don't try to trap each other in small games or roles that don't serve the other person's being. When authenticity rules, we have profoundly supportive and mutually empowering relationships which lay the groundwork for loving families and societies. A truly free human being wishes to honor their agreements without entering into slavery agreements or, as my father's friend Bill Garland wryly and astutely called them, "Domestic Incarceration Partnerships."

Domestic incarceration is a metaphor for the way many of us have entrapped both our partners and ourselves in patterns of trying to be a certain way. These relationships become like a prison where we cannot be free to fully be ourselves.

Story: *The Honest Lover*

When I realized my former fiancé was judging me, I told her how I felt. She didn't understand what I was talking about and denied my feelings. The closer we got to getting married, the more controlling she became.

When I ended the engagement, it broke her heart. It wasn't an easy process, but it was the honest way to end the domestic incarceration she had set in motion.

I tried desperately to reach her, but she refused to open up to me. I had let her into the deepest places in my heart, and she had the potential to know me in a way no one had ever known me before. The betrayal of being so close and then having her turn against me in judgment felt like too much for my heart to bear. This is the path of learning that I took to come out of a relationship which was not serving me anymore.

I became filled with rage at the injustice and cruelty she was coming from. She had none of the kindness, sweetness, and care she had previously embodied.

If she had simply said, "I need to go another way, but thank you for our exploration," we could have let each other go with love. I would never have denied her authentic expression. Judgments and condemnation are not authentic. When she told me I was wrong for being how I was being, I had to take a stand against her judgmental lies.

This is the story of how our relationship dissolved and how I found a deeper layer of love. In the end, even with all the pain of this breakup, I'm grateful I was honest with her and stayed true to my heart.

Straight Words: *Be Honest With Your Lover*

Tell your lover how you really feel and what's on your heart and mind. There's no reason to hide what you feel. When we are afraid we will hurt other people's feelings with our authenticity, we are actually hurting ourselves. If who you really are hurts your partner, you may not be a right fit. Don't let yourself be in something that traps you. Be honest and let the chips fall where they may. It's better to be single than caught in a relationship trap that limits who you are.

Game: *Free Yourself From the Relationship Trap*

1. Turn your attention to the relationships in your life that are the most important to you. Take on a playful attitude, as if you're looking at them while doing a summersault or headstand.

2. If you are in a romantic relationship, notice all the little places you feel trapped trying to be a certain way for your partner. If you are single, remember the last time you were in a relationship and tried to be different for your partner.

3. What is the most playful way to get out of pressuring yourself to be a certain way? One possibility is for you to pressure yourself even more to be a certain way for your partner. With your imagination, exaggerate it and make yourself be exactly who you think they want you to be.

4. Feel the pressure in it. Now let it go.

5. Notice the futile absurdity of trying to be different from your nature.

6. What if you got to be authentically yourself in the relationship? Imagine what that would feel like. Notice where you feel this in your body.

7. Let yourself just be how you are—whether you are single, in a relationship, alone, or with others. Release all of the pressure.

8. Simply let yourself be.

9. Notice any ways you've tried to pressure your current partner (or past partners) to be different from how they are.

10. Let them also be themselves. Even if you don't want to be with this person as they are, it's better to let them be themselves.

11. Now let yourself be you, and let them be them. Relax, breathe, and embrace things as they are.

35 Authenticity in Friendship

The transcendentalists paved the way for me to understand the ethic of authentic friendship. Poet and essayist Ralph Waldo Emerson described the kinds of friendships he seeks in his essay "Self-Reliance"–a true friend is one who is undomesticated by society, who speaks the rude truth, and relies on the Self. This kind of self-reliance is necessary for true authenticity in friendship, and is imperative for authenticity everywhere. He talks about speaking the "rude truth" to people who are out of integrity. In our modern world, it can be easy to settle for polite friends who tell us what we want to hear. However, true friends tell us what is true. They do not mince words. They speak their minds and their hearts with integrity and truth.

Story: *An Inauthentic Friend*

Ben was one of my best friends for the first year or two of college. He helped me loosen my social inhibitions. We would make a scene wherever and whenever we felt so moved. I distinctly remember Ben inspiring me to stand on top of the tables in the dining hall with him as we belted out our dramatic rendition of "I Will Survive" by Gloria

Gaynor so everyone who was in the food court couldn't help but be entertained by us. We had so much fun in those early days of college. Ben was spontaneous, creative, playful, and charming. I was always true to the friendship, but Ben turned out to be an inauthentic friend to me. Ben had a friend named Joe who had a tendency towards extreme arrogance. This is where my tension with Ben first began.

Joe and I started arguing over his condescending tone in reply to my interpretation of the Shakespeare play, *Twelfth Night*. This escalated to a wrestling match outside the dormitory. After this fight, Joe and I were okay with each other. However, things were never the same with Ben.

Ben never told me why he turned away from our friendship. I suspect he formed some false conclusion about me after witnessing my authentic anger with Joe's narcissistic tendencies. (Joe later discovered he was a narcissist and wrote an article about his path to recovery.)

Even though Ben turned on me, I continue to stay true to our friendship. I wish him and his family all the best in all the days of their lives. I hope one day Ben and I might spend some time together in true friendship again, romping around the Dartmouth Campus.

Straight Words: *Tell the Truth*

Be courageous and tell the truth. Don't let fear sway you in friendship. If you're afraid you'll lose a friend if you're honest, you need to ask how good the friendship really is. I'm not talking about honesty as an excuse for selfish or cruel behavior. There are many people who hide behind the excuse of authenticity to be mean and project onto others. I'm talking about saying what's in your heart to say. When your friend turns out to be false, it breaks your heart. There's so much we can learn from the heartbreak of betrayal.

Game: *Honesty in Friendship*

1. Find a courageous friend who's open to real honesty.

2. Touch your hand to your heart and open up to this friend. Invite them into a complete honesty game. Tell them how you really feel. You can tell them what you appreciate about them, what you don't like about them, or both.

3. Say whatever is on your heart to say. Be completely honest about whatever you feel.

4. Take turns, letting them do the same for you.

5. Continue with the flow of conversation in whatever way feels right.

6. Reflect on how it was for you. How did you feel? What did you learn?

7. Keep practicing this kind of honesty as best you can as you move into other relationships and connections in your day and throughout your life.

SECTION III: Authenticity Under Fire

I've always been authentic. My authenticity has caused immense conflict, strife, and beauty in my life. The path I've taken to walk in an authentic way has been quite radical. For a time, I needed to be able to say what was true in my heart to anyone at any time. This authenticity was forged from the fires of deep trauma.

While in the cult, I held my true authentic self back out of fear that I would hurt other people. After I awoke from the cult, I refused to hold back in any way and initially railed against anything that reminded me of the narcissistic oppression I had suffered. These conflicts were like the fires that open up the seeds of a redwood tree and allow them to blossom into their full blown, authentic nature.[12]

Section III highlights the ways our conflict-averse society represses authenticity. Our society would rather have us be polite and tolerate lies than be authentic and risk conflict. Conflict can clear the

---

[12] Redwood trees need fire to open their seeds. Fire helps them to reproduce.

path and bring healing. Conflict is like a storm that shakes up and disturbs the status quo.

Authentic conflict is clarifying. It shows you where you are with another person. Most of the conflicts I've gotten into are with people who were embodying narcissistic behavioral patterns they were unaware of and unwilling to look at. Narcissism creates a lot of confusion for those who are touched by it. I believe that when we crack the code of narcissistic dysfunction, we will have a society that truly works for everyone.

In my first attempt at a book about authenticity, the subtitle was "The Power to Be Yourself in a World Full of Lies," which really means the power to be yourself in a world full of narcissism. Narcissism is the essential type of lying that separates us from ourselves and each other. When I woke up to the fact that what I thought had been a tight knit spiritual community was actually a cult run by a narcissist, I felt liberated. But gradually, I began to realize that our society's dominant culture is a narcissistic cult in the sense that it is dedicated to self-interest and the enhancement of the ego over the being. Social media, our economy, and the way we relate to success all encourage, reinforce, and celebrate narcissism.

After coming out of the cult I was in for 18 years, I was literally mad as hell at anyone who was being oppressive. I wasn't going to take it or allow it anymore. I was cursed and gifted with narcissistic trauma. Poetically, I like to say I was touched by evil. Narcissistic trauma wounded me deeply, yet at the same time it opened my eyes to my purpose and mission. This trauma helped me see inauthenticity, narcissism, and cruelty in many mundane interactions. Whenever people lacked empathy and judged others in small ways, I became incensed. I couldn't help but fight people with a radical intensity.

In this section, each story about a conflict is a true tale of my path to awakening. It took great courage to stand my ground and speak my truth in many of these situations. As I reflect on these specific situations, I am aware of the many ways in which I would handle these conflicts differently if they were happening today.

No matter how angry I was, I always held my adversaries in love. I want nothing more than to melt the ice in their hearts and have true love prevail on earth. This is my dream for all my relations.[13]

Everyone has their own style and way of being authentic. I hope some of these stories inspire your style of being authentically, truly, and outrageously yourself.

---

13 "All my relations" is the way the Lakota Sioux tribe start and end their prayers. In their language they say, "*Mitakuye oyasin*." This way of thinking about all the relations is practiced among many indigenous tribes of North America.

36 Conflict Can Be Necessary

Authenticity does not shy away from conflict. It does not seek conflict either. Rather, it welcomes necessary conflict. Necessary conflict is the conflict that comes from being true to yourself as opposed to the conflict that comes from aggrandizing or defending your ego. In my experience, our authentic being does not like unnecessary conflict. Unnecessary conflict is conflict that arises from trying to control another person or situation. Conflict can also arise from unnecessary competition with another person.

Creating conflict in this way is part of life and part of the learning journey. When we get lost in fear, we simply want to return to love as soon as we can. It's good to create as few unnecessary conflicts as possible. However once the conflict is created, it has become part of the path you've chosen to learn from. If you realize you've created unnecessary conflict, simply take responsibility for what is unconscious in you and apologize.

Story: *Authentic Conflict*

At Bridging Worlds, we practice empathy and unconditional love with our staff as well as our clients. One employee became critical and judgmental after being promoted to a managerial position. She began to hold grudges and act in a way that was creating unnecessary conflict with the staff. I told her that she could not continue in the position unless she stopped leading with hateful and judgmental energy.

She walked out of the meeting and I walked after her. She began to yell at me about how awful of a person I was. She spewed lies and venom in a way that was meant to hurt me. I held my ground and yelled back at her. She escalated further by striking me in the head with her hands. When I told her I was going to call the police, she collapsed to the floor in what appeared to be a contrite apology. We talked it through and seemed to be getting back on track.

One week later, she said that I was to blame for the situation by running at her and scaring her. She claimed that she was acting in self-defense. I saw through her lies and didn't take them personally. After this experience, I had first hand knowledge of the emotional abuse and manipulations the staff were telling me about.

Samantha the CEO and I stood firm with the values of the company and did everything we could to support this manager in finding her way back to our values. She kept resorting to blame and eventually resigned. Soon after her resignation, we were able to bring more cohesion to our staff culture by sharing with everyone what had transpired. I'm glad I took a stand for the values and I'm grateful that she is no longer at the company. I learned a lot from her about how important it is for me to stand my ground against this kind of divisiveness.

Hatred cannot be allowed to rule if love is what you're after. The fires of her hatred helped me learn to love more. As I stood my ground with her, four other people who were embodying narcissistic tendencies fell away from my life. I was leveling up.

Straight Words: *Embrace Authentic Conflict*

Don't let others push you around. When there's an authentic conflict to be had, stand true and be bold. Follow your heart in all things and do what truly feels right. Others will think what they think. You cannot control that. Just stay true to yourself.

You have control over how you respond to the conflict. You have no control over how they respond. You may have a greater understanding of the conflict later. You don't have to be right or prove a point. It's okay to be where you are and speak your truth. If you can avoid the conflict while being true to yourself, always do that. If authenticity demands the conflict, embrace it.

Conflict is much like a storm. Sometimes it rains with thunder and lightning before it passes. The Sun will always shine again. I believe that peace will always prevail no matter how bad the conflict is. Sometimes this peace comes soon after the conflict, and other times it may take many years or even lifetimes before some conflicts are resolved.

Game: *Authentic Conflict*

1. Find a friend you trust—someone you can practice authentic conflict with.

2. Find some place where there's authentic grounds for disagreement or slight conflict.

3. Have an agreement that you are going to lean into the conflict with the love you feel for each other. That love is what will support the whole thing underneath, much like a rock climber uses a belay to support them as they climb.[14]

---

[14] A belay is the rope system rock climbers use, which is there to catch the climber if they fall.

4. Express what you feel while using empathy with the other person.

5. Let them express what they feel and use empathy for them.

6. Learn what you can out of the conflict. Don't defend your ego. Just let in whatever the other says unless they are unfairly attacking you or not speaking the truth. (If they are unfairly attacking you, state that without defensiveness, as best you can.)

7. Assuming you've resolved things in a good way, thank them for the conflict and the opportunity to learn together.

8. If you haven't resolved things, thank them (or the universe) for bringing you this painful learning opportunity. If you aren't able to feel gratitude for the unresolved conflict, simply accept whatever you feel. *Note*: For those you're not on speaking terms with, simply practice with a friend or act it out yourself.

37 Societal Laws and Fear

The rules and laws of our society often enforce inauthentic politeness and rule-following over realness. We are conditioned to believe that human nature is vile, and must be controlled and trained to keep us from becoming "like animals." The truth is that we are animals. Returning to our natural state would heal many of the problems in our society including rape, murder, and torture. In my observation, when people are in a natural state of connection, they don't intentionally hurt each other.

We obviously need to prevent people from raping and murdering each other while humanity is in its current stage of development. But what is driving people to act this way? The simple answer is trauma. Our current society causes a lot of unnecessary trauma. Many of our actions are unconsciously motivated by our past traumas. When we actually deal with the issues in our society by creating healthy families and communities of support, we will significantly reduce trauma and in turn the crime rate will decrease.

We need proactive solutions to identify at-risk individuals and support them before they commit crimes. Almost everyone who rapes and murders shows signs of this behavior in childhood or sometime before the act happens. Often, these behaviors start with cruelty to animals and violence in the home. Many of these behaviors stem from an extreme lack of empathy. As parents and educators, we need to be honest about these warning signs and seek support to prevent unnecessary suffering.

When we have a truly empathic and loving society, we don't need laws to artificially hold people in place. The guiding principles and agreements of empathy and unconditional love would replace the police state and the criminal industrial complex we now have. It's my understanding that all people who commit crimes have some sort of emotional trauma and are unconsciously calling out for love and support. We need to love and support each other and transform the culture to match the shape of our own heart.

Story: *Standing Up to Laws Coming From Fear*

I have many stories where I have spoken out and stood up to authorities. It's always been my superpower to defend against injustice and inauthenticity in my local world. I fiercely defended my friend Chris in high school when DJ was bullying him and calling him racist names. In another situation, I fiercely defended myself and all autistic people when a therapist judged and refused to help me with emotional regulation after I demonstrated the issues I came to see her for. I even fought a battle with a martial arts instructor who was hateful toward transgender people and compared Marx to Hitler. While I believe these instances of taking a stand against authority have been important, they have had a minimal impact beyond my personal victory and have sometimes resulted in alienation within the community.

The story of Rosa Parks is iconic for taking a stand. Rosa Parks had a headache and would not give up her seat to the white passengers as was required by the law in Montgomery, Alabama in 1955. The three African American riders next to her gave up their seats while she refused. She was arrested. The stand that she took ignited the community. She said that she was tired. She wasn't just tired physically, she was tired in her heart and soul at the grave injustices of racism. She is considered the mother of the civil rights movement and paved the way for the work of other great leaders like Martin Luther King Jr.

We can all admire Rosa Parks as an exemplar of authenticity. All the little opportunities to act against tyrannical laws must be fought for. We never know the true impact of each act we perform. We may one day inspire an authenticity revolution by simply being ourselves.

Straight Words: *Welcome Anger*

Anger is the emotion that often brings attention to and calls out grave injustice. When anger comes from your pure heart, it takes a stand for truth. Anger has been deeply judged against in our society. Accept all your anger and let yourself feel it fully and completely when it comes. Get mad at the things that make you mad, and let yourself fully express that anger. When you feel the righteous injustices of society around you acting on you, be authentic even when the rules and customs of society judge against this realness.

Don't hurt other people with your anger or act out violently in any way unless you need to act in self-defense. Simply take a stand for what feels right for you. Just as Rosa Parks did, we too can take a stand for truth, love, and justice.

Game: *'Unrule' Yourself*

1. Notice whatever rule you've internalized that tells you to control your own behavior.

2. Notice how this rule is being held in your mind. Notice how this rule exists because you are afraid of acting naturally in some way.

3. Feel the fear you would feel if you were to let go of this rule.

4. Find the energy of this fear in your body. Is it warm or cool, hard or soft, tight or loose, sharp or dull, moving or still?

5. Bring complete acceptance to the energy.

6. Let go of the rule and allow yourself to be without it.

7. Notice how it feels to let go of this limiting rule.

8. Trust in your natural response to do what's right, without rules in your mind dictating your behavior.

9. Notice what happens as you live your life without "shoulds" or "have to's."

10. Trust in your own ability to discern what is right for you. By trusting your unruly self who knows no rules, you can truly rule your world.

38 *Authenticity Can Be Offensive*

We must not live our lives enslaved by what other people think. Being who we are is an act of revolution! Authenticity doesn't wait for others to accept us. We simply are as we are. When the clouds rain down on the earth, they don't ask for permission. When an ocean wave breaks on the shoreline, when lightning strikes a tree, when a volcano erupts, and when the earth quakes—none of these forces ask for permission. We are a force of nature and we are meant to be this way. We are not meant to beg permission or seek approval from others. We are like a star, a sun, or a great storm.

Where I live in Northern California, it has become customary to ask permission before speaking your truth to someone or giving them feedback. In some situations this may be called for and beneficial. However, a culture in which we have to ask permission to be ourselves is an inauthentic culture.

In my experience, the ideology of the political far left can embody a similar kind of hatred as the far right. The far right often takes discriminatory positions based on race, gender, sexual preference, and socioeconomic status. The far left often takes extreme care as to not offend anyone. When people enforce politically correct (PC) rules which do not allow others to authentically express themselves, we have another kind of authoritarian police state.

The #MeToo movement was helpful in outing sexual abuse and injustice. However, it also fed this idea that people can be canceled. This act of canceling people is another form of hatred. Free speech is essential to having a free society. Hate speech that incites violence against people is not free speech and must be called out and checked. The PC movement seeks to control our speech with a kind of "newspeak" akin to what is used in *1984,* George Orwell's dystopian novel.

When we are authentic to what is in our heart, the words we use matter less than the feelings in our heart. The stand that we need to take is against hatred and discrimination, not against certain kinds of words which could be interpreted as offensive. To be clear, I stand with supporting all people and ending discrimination. However, we cannot end discrimination with emotional violence that lacks empathy. The left and the right need to stop enacting emotional violence toward each other and the people they disagree with. We must allow everyone to be themselves and we must be honest with them about how we feel. Let's replace "cancel culture" with a culture of authentic empathy and love.

Story: *Offensive Authenticity*

I had a staff meeting in which I was ostracized for speaking my truth. The day before this staff meeting I found out a friend of mine had been raped by someone else in our local community. The news weighed heavily on my heart. In our staff meetings we had a practice of each of us personally sharing about what we were feeling and what was going on in our lives before getting down to business. As a rule, anything was welcome. I shared how affected I was by my friend's experience of being raped. I shared my grief and anger and expressed my desire to bring an end to rape in our society.

Many of the staff did not understand where I was coming from. I wasn't seen as an ally who was visioning a world and society in which women were no longer abused and these horrific acts no longer existed. Instead, I was seen as a man and boss who was engaging in abuse through talking about rape without consent. One staff member even suggested that my way of talking about this was some kind of exploitative state where I was getting power through sharing my friend's story and feeding off of the energy. Several staff members felt justified in openly judging and attacking my authentic expression. I told the staff members, "If this is the kind of empathy you offer your clients, I don't think you should work here."

They took even deeper umbrage at my statement, responding by saying I was threatening their jobs. The truth was I was simply sharing the authentic truth I felt in the moment.

After the meeting, I talked things over with my managers. The managers sided with the staff members' allegations that I was being inappropriate. I withdrew from leading the company for a period of time and reflected on whether my conduct at the staff meeting was inappropriate or unbecoming of a leader. I wanted to do everything I could to make the staff members feel comfortable and it seemed as though my behavior was setting them off. After several months of reflection, I began to realize how untrue these allegations were. I was being discriminated against for my authenticity. I could not allow this kind of hatred and discrimination to happen at the company toward me or anyone else. I took a stand.

I filed a formal complaint with my managers against several staff as an employee who believed they were being discriminated against. My managers told me I couldn't do that. I said, "Yes I can. I'm an employee and an owner and I don't want to use my owner privilege to address this. I'd rather you both support me as an employee who is being discriminated against based on gender perspectives and racial misperceptions." Certain members of my staff kept telling me I was a white man. I'm non-white as my father is from South Africa with roots going back to India. At that time, I wasn't identifying as a man, but exploring a polygender identity in which I was both a man and a woman and neither a man nor a woman. Further detail on that exploration would require more explanation than this book allows.

My managers refused to accept my formal complaint, so I dealt with it as the owner. First, I set a boundary with my managers. If they couldn't stop discriminating against me and condemning me for my authenticity, then they could no longer be at the company. I had several conversations with them. These conversations resulted in one resignation and one termination. Next, I held ground by drawing a line in the sand with the staff when I declared that hatred, judgments, and condemnation would not be allowed in our staff meetings or staff culture. I said, "You will practice empathy and unconditional love or you can get the fuck out." At the time, I could not stand this kind of behavior. I also said, "If you want to keep practicing judgmental behavior, there are many other companies that will tolerate it." Bridging Worlds took a fierce stand for empathy and unconditional love. We had already taken this stand with our clients, but now we were also doing it with each other.

Samantha became the new CEO. She led the way to making a company culture that truly worked for everyone with my support and assistance. Together, we reshaped the company into a more fully empathic and loving community. While the judgment and condemnation from many staff was inappropriate, there was a legitimate concern some were expressing about being forced into deep emotional processes. The way we were structuring the check-ins were not wholly supportive of the company and staff, so we addressed this by reshaping staff meetings and making them more focused on the clients and our work together. This made a more safe and inclusive space for everyone. We reserved most of the deeper emotional processes for the managers' group.

The new dynamic has led our company to flourish with the most deeply aligned staff we have ever had. I'm so grateful we went through the fires of these experiences. We have a much better sense of our values and culture through these important lessons. We have a culture in which conflict is welcome and we work it through together, using the conflict to continue learning and growing. While we still have a hierarchical structure with Samantha at the helm and the other managers supporting the staff, we recognize that we are all equal as human beings. This underlying equality is what drives our company culture and makes us feel like a truly loving family.

Straight Words: *Be True to Yourself Even if It's Offensive to Others*

It's okay to be viewed as offensive when you're being authentic. It's also okay to soften your words so that your communication lands better. I've learned over time that the whole truth is often too much for most people to bear. It's okay to lose friends who cannot handle the truth. This kind of truth-telling will change your life because you are staying true to yourself. Those who can't handle the truth of you living in your fullness will naturally fall away from you.

Here's how you do it. First you find what feels truly authentic. Next, find the best way you have available to communicate this. However it comes out, don't judge it. Listen and learn from the response you get. Simply refine it through practice and experience. You want to listen most to your heart and feel for what feels right to you and what feels like it needs more refinement.

Game: *Making Offensive Authenticity Smooth*

1. Start with a friend who can handle honesty and see if they would like to play this game with you. Drop into rapport with them by first opening your heart to them and then using empathy to put yourself in their shoes.

2. Let them know you're going to practice saying something they might perceive as offensive. Get consent.

3. State the raw, naked truth of what you observe in this person. It could be as direct as this statement: "In my perception, when it comes to romance, you seem to lie to yourself and hurt yourself with some of the unconscious choices you make."

4. Now say it again but differently. Keep the truth in it, but soften its impact by changing your tone or softening the words while maintaining the underlying message. It could be, "When you talk with me about your romantic life, it feels like you sometimes get lost in fantasy and can't tell what's really happening in the dynamics."

5. Be in as much empathic rapport with the person as possible as you are saying it, while also being honest with them.

6. Compare the two ways of expressing yourself with your friend and get feedback on how each one felt.

7. Now try it with an acquaintance. This time, do not do it the most direct, extreme way first. Instead, start with the level of direct authenticity you think they will be able to handle in the flow of the conversation. It could be as simple as, "you seem a little distracted and not connected right now. What are you experiencing?"

39 The Inauthenticity of Trying

Trying to do something or be like someone else puts us in a position of unnatural effort, control, and inauthenticity. It's different from striving to learn something. I love learning. I want to learn to be better at playing music, opening my heart, and living in authenticity. I'm not approaching any of these areas from the place where there's anything wrong with me. I just have a desire to be better at them all.

When we "try," we struggle against who we are. We may look to someone else and try to be more like them. It's wonderful to be inspired by others. However, trying to be just like them is a betrayal to yourself. You were meant to be how you were meant to be. If you were meant to be them, you would have been born as them. You were born as you. Open to this and don't attempt to be any different. Learning from others is wonderful and natural, but don't try to be them.

Story: *Anti-Trying*

I spent many years studying under a teacher who was masterful at coaching and teaching others. He was a gifted facilitator who founded Process Coaching—a synthesis of hypnotherapy, NLP

(Neuro-linguistic programming), and psychic awareness skills. I admired him immensely. But I was so afraid of being myself that I modeled my behavior after his. He encouraged me to speak, write, approach my business, format documents, choose girlfriends, and facilitate groups just as he did.

I spent 16 of the 18 years I studied with him trying to be like him. I criticized myself when I did things my way and not his way. The process of not being myself was excruciating. Eventually, I had to stop this foolish trying game.

This story is called anti-trying because it showed me how much trying to be someone else was a violation of my own being. If I was meant to be him, I would not have been born as myself.

Many people beat themselves up for having been in a cult. I don't regret the experiences I have had. I see them as a necessary part of my awakening journey. Being trapped in a cult and getting out is how I learned to reclaim my authentic way of being. Before I got out, I believed there was something wrong with me. This made me susceptible to mind control tactics. The way I was had to be wrong, so I was trying to be someone else. If learning from my experience can save you any time, I would suggest we all simply be ourselves and stop trying to be anyone else. Being who you are is the greatest gift you can offer the world.

Straight Words: *Stop Trying!*

"I'm tired of trying. It's full of bullshit," are words my friend and former partner, Heather, improvised in a song we sang together. Her words still ring true to this day. There's no need to try to be any way other than the way you are. Trying only leads to inauthenticity. Any time you put pressure on yourself or stress around how you are being, it is a clear sign that you are trying. Simply notice it, relax, and return to a more natural state of being.

While it's good to learn from others, always stay true to who you are. You are the way you are for a reason. You dishonor yourself when you try to be different. Always honor yourself. Always honor your being. Embrace the magical and wondrous you.

Game: *Trying and Allowing*

1. Take a simple task like washing a dish or picking up a fork. It can be anything you want.

2. Perform the task as usual in the natural way you do it.

3. Now, try really hard and make it as difficult as possible through trying. Have fun with it as you make it extra hard.

4. Now let go of trying. Simply allow yourself to do it as effortlessly as possible.

5. Notice how it feels to simply allow.

6. Now try to be a different person from who you are. Pick a person in the world you admire and try to be them in your imagination.

7. While it can be good to place yourself in their shoes when learning or using empathy, notice how it feels to try to make yourself be different by being them.

8. Now let that go and simply be yourself again.

9. Keep allowing and letting go of any trying as you move through your day and embrace your own unique style.

40 Being Yourself is Who You Are Meant to Be

You were born to be a certain way in this world. If you were meant to be someone else, you would have been born as them. You were meant to share your unique gifts. There's a mass delusion in humanity that there's something wrong with us. It's embedded in the ego of each person.

The ego hates itself. It has a built-in self-hating mechanism. When we believe the lie that there's something wrong with us, we start trying to be who we are not. Only when we dedicate our ego to our deeper being can we overcome this hatred. We must face it, accept it, and not embody it. Through dedicating the ego in service to the whole, we naturally embody love and become who we are meant to be.

Story: *Being Myself in the Face of Great Adversity*

When I first realized the group I was in was a cult, I started telling my closest friends and colleagues in the group what I was noticing. They fought me and tried to tell me that I was projecting my own issues onto the leader. I told them that what they were saying was part of the cult's mind control technique to keep them trapped. When you turn all the feedback someone is giving back on them, you can control the narrative. This process of deflecting feedback is part of the narcissistic strategy called DARVO.[15]

My closest friends in the group refused to budge and continued to believe I was wrong. I wrote emails, made phone calls, and stood my ground. Everyone told me that I was wrong and that I needed to work on myself or change my attitude. They tried to suck me back into the cult lingo and frame the story as if the leader had to be right. I eventually spoke to someone who was not in the cult's inner circle. It turned out that she had tried to leave the day before I spoke with her. The cult leader had talked her back into staying. I told her, "If you want to leave, you can leave." In that five minute telephone conversation she was freed.

After that conversation with her, I spoke with two other members who immediately saw how manipulative and toxic the leader was. Soon the

---

[15] Deny, Attack, Reverse Victim Offender Relations is a strategy that narcissists use to deflect the truth, gaslight, and avoid taking responsibility, developed by Jennifer Freyd. It exists in politics, workplaces, family situations, and anywhere else you can find narcissism.

ripple effect took hold. A week from the first successful conversation, I wrote an email titled "cults and sociopaths," which exposed many of the lies of the group.

I later told the leader he wasn't fit to lead our group anymore and that I wouldn't allow him to hurt us. We had a text exchange in which I told him I was taking the class from him. Because I had the truth on my side and so much experience in the group, I was able to help others see the light and return to themselves. It was still a long path to recovery for all of us, but since that day we have been free of his abuse and mind control.

My former fiancé and other friends encouraged me to give up on the other group members and save myself. I said, "They are like my family. I can't leave them there." I'm so grateful that I followed my heart and faced the challenge to help liberate everyone from the cult.

I was almost able to reach the leader and help him free himself from his deep abuse patterns. The perpetrators of abuse are trapped just as their victims are. We are all in need of healing. My deepest prayer for him is that he finds the healing he needs to see the light of truth and open his heart to real love. He ended up having a psychotic episode and was temporarily institutionalized. When he got out of the institution, he doubled down on the belief that I was starting a rival cult to his and exercising a personal vendetta against him. It's my hope that one day he realizes how much I still love him. May he come to see that everything I did for the group was also an act of love for him.

Straight Words: *Always Be Yourself!*

"To be yourself is all that you can do," are very telling lyrics from the band Audioslave's song "Be Yourself." Take a stand by being true to yourself. You may not be as popular as you once were. Some people will tell you to conform to the norms of society. Ignore them and stay true to your own values. Let go of the need to be popular and liked. Simply be yourself and let the chips fall where they may. Trust, let go, and be yourself. Those who truly love you will stand by your side.

Game: *Be Yourself*

1. Turn your attention to yourself and enjoy your own particular quality of attention. No one in the world has ever had the same quality of attention you have. It's like a fingerprint; your attention is uniquely you.

2. Notice the quality of your attention. Is it fluid like water? Is it steady like a rock? Or does it move like a butterfly, flitting from one thing

to the other? What is the shape of its path? Is it linear, circular, does it spiral, or is it something else?

3. Touch your heart and feel it beat. Notice what it feels like to be inside your heart.

4. Notice that there are "instructions" inside you for how to live. These instructions are inscribed right here in your nature. Your heart tells you what you feel about each and every situation.

5. Trust how you were meant to be and let everything fall into place.

6. Let go of any trying to be different. Just breathe it out.

7. Breathe in acceptance of yourself as you are.

8. Continue letting yourself be as your true nature desires.

9. Let your attention move how it moves. Let your mind think how it thinks. Let your heart feel how it feels.

41 Inauthenticity is Born Out of Fear

All inauthenticity comes from fear. Typically, fear tells us that we will not be lovable if we are ourselves. This makes us try to be someone else. Fear is so rampant that most of us walk around not knowing we are being inauthentic. We are so used to conforming to some way we think we are supposed to be that we often forget we are conforming at all.

Story: *The Inauthentic Leader*

I had an employee in a leadership role for many years. She was amazingly intelligent and an exceptional communicator with many great clinical skills and capacities. However, she couldn't handle my authenticity and was afraid of me. I saw it many times and asked her about it. She denied that she was afraid of me. Whenever she became judgemental of me, I supported her time and time again. She would say she had moved through her issues and everything was okay. Yet, she would return back to the same fear and distrust. She seemed to live from her fear. I believe she was afraid that I would fire her if I knew how she really felt about me.

Once I recognized what was going on, I spent a full year doing everything I could to find an authentic way of relating with her that felt good for both of us. I could not coax her out of her loyalty to her fear. The only solution which remained was for her to leave the company. We could have moved through this in another way had she been willing to be authentic and actually tell me how she felt.

Fear does not allow for things to move. Fear keeps us trapped in inauthenticity. Through working with her for over five years, I learned about the nuances of fear. In many ways, her fear was similar to my former fiancé's fear. Their fear and hatred was so subtle I didn't notice it at first. Both of them taught me how to detect the most subtle forms of divisive energy.

Straight Words: *Stop Acting from Fear*

Humanity stands on a dangerous precipice caused by taking unconscious actions from fear. Stop any action motivated by fear. The heart does not choose fear. The heart always chooses love. When we open the heart to love, we can love the fear. When we live from the heart, we are not moved to do anything motivated by unconscious fear. It's too late in the game for humanity to be run by fear. As they said in New Jersey where I grew up, it's too late for us to be "chickenshit, spoiled, little egotistical brats." Humanity is capable of *so much more* when we come from love and not fear. Open your eyes, wake up, and love one another. Open your heart and use empathy in all your relations.

Game*: Play with Fear*

1. Playfully notice where you are closed off in fear. Signs of fear include slight anxiety in the heart, a sense of dread, or feeling like bad things are going to happen. Fear can also manifest as a general feeling of stress or excessive thinking.

2. Feel the fear in your body. What does it feel like?

3. Notice if there is any desire to hide the fear or pretend it's not there.

4. Fear tends to make us want to be inauthentic. Don't let it trap you—just acknowledge it, call it out, and continue to play with it.

5. Dance with fear and own it while you feel it.

6. Allow its energy to flow inside of you without trying to push it away. We all have fears. There's no shame in that.

7. Allow your fears to be here as they are without trying to move off of them.

8. They will not always be with you. Enjoy them while they are here.

42 Taking a Stand

Before I encountered narcissism up close, I was not as fierce in my convictions. I thought humanity was generally kind and loving, and I did not understand why we had all the problems that exist in the world. After suffering from narcissistic wounding at the hands of a cult leader, my former fiancé, and many other people in business and friendship, I realized why we have so many problems in humanity.

In short, it all comes down to divisive energy. Divisive energy is the energy which divides us. It can exist within oneself in the form of self-criticism and self-judgment. It can be targeted at others in the form of blaming and judging.

An authentic heart gets angry at any divisive energy. Our heart cannot stomach this energy. Our heart wouldn't ask our stomach to endure anything that doesn't feel good to it. When we take a stand against divisive energy, we don't allow it to rule our world, our self, or any of our relationships.

Narcissists often align with divisive energy. They use it to generate power. My former mentor judged and blamed me and others to get control. My former fiancé was more subtle about it, but she also used condemnation to prove her righteousness.

Narcissists are always covering up a central lie that causes disconnection. Narcissists hide their essential nature with lies about who they are and who they want to be. They deceive others creating a sense of disconnection between their self-image and their true selves. This pattern creates disconnection in all their relations. This disconnection can be masked by the power of their charisma, charm, and manipulative strategies.

My former mentor believed that others couldn't understand him because he was so special. Because he did not want to sincerely feel his wound, he became grandiose.

My former fiancé had difficulties forming friendships. She struggled being alone with herself. She admitted to many of her flaws and yet she blamed others for her problems as a means to hide her true dysfunction. In this way, she displayed the characteristics of a vulnerable or covert narcissist. She was not grandiose. Rather, she used narcissistic tactics to subtly criticize and control me into being the kind of boyfriend she wanted. When I didn't conform to her jealousy, she would withdraw her love and make me the cause of her problems.

Story: *Standing Against Divisive People*

There are more stories about my stands against divisive people than I have space for in this book. In retrospect, divisiveness has continuously and relentlessly brought me into deeper levels of love.

You've already heard a lot about the two most divisive people in my life, my former fiancé and my former mentor from the cult. In many ways, my mentor is by far the most divisive person I have ever met. He systematically tried to make me into a carbon copy of himself. He was so hopelessly lost in his wounding that he had no awareness of the control strategies he lived his life from. He is what licensed social worker and cult recovery expert Dan Shaw calls a traumatizing narcissist. He surrounded himself with people he could abuse and feed off of energetically.

I experienced this first hand by studying under him for 18 years. When I spoke my truth to him, he threw me out of the group and attempted to get me to "donate" my shares of the business back to him and the other business partners. His actions showed a fundamental lack of integrity. I experienced him engaging in several lies to protect his image. He accused me of not embodying the healing work we were doing and not being authentic. But in fact, he was the one who was out of integrity with the work and his own heart.

He should never have been a mentor to others. His method was to make people "fix" themselves. The truth is, there is nothing needing to be fixed in any of us. The wounds that I suffered from, by being in his cult, will take me a long time to heal. Although I learned vital skills and had important experiences, I lost myself deeply and profoundly. I trusted in him more than I trusted myself. I would have done nearly anything he told me because I believed he was truly looking out for my best interest. I was sure he was wiser than I would ever be. When I realized he was simply out for himself and using all of us, my world nearly shattered.

Piecing myself together from this trauma has made me the kind of person I am today. American essayist Ralph Waldo Emerson in his Essay on Self Reliance says something to the effect that, "A weak man is made by his experience and a strong man makes himself out of his experience."[16] Writing this book is part of my attempt to piece myself back together from this wounding. Like in the Japanese process of Kintsugi, I'm taking the imperfections and cracks in my emotional body and bringing

---

[16] We haven't been able to find the origins of this thought, but Adam believes it is attributed to Ralph Waldo Emerson in his essay *Self-Reliance*. This thought applies equally to women and all genders.

them together with gold. Through honoring these wounds, I find deeper love for myself and for life. The wounds I suffered with my mother's breakdown when I was four and a half set me on the course to unlock my empathy and unfold my potential. If you had told me in my teenage years this wounding was a gift, I would have had no idea what you were talking about. I can see with age that each wound brings yet another set of gifts. I eagerly await the harvesting of all the gifts that will come from this cult wound.

————

My former fiancé is another story entirely. She is so sweet to everyone that no one would ever suspect the dangers that lie beneath her sweet facade. This is called covert narcissism.

When we have an open heart, we want to believe in the goodness of others, especially when we love them. I blamed myself for nearly two years over the loss of this relationship. The more time that passes, the more I realize how I was subtly and covertly abused and manipulated for much of the relationship.

When we bond closely with someone who engages in these patterns, there's a trauma bond which forms. This trauma bond can be very addictive.

Narcissistic people are capable of making us feel like the most special people in the world. Since they know how special they want to be treated, they can be incredibly gifted at showering us with "feel good" attention. This is often called love bombing in the sense that it is a manipulative weapon and not true love. When they withdraw this special kind of "love," we can often feel lost without this special attention.

I sincerely wish her and my former mentor well and thank them both for deepening my love. I pray for them and hope they find healing for these deep-seated wounds. There's goodness and love in both of them and they deserve my unconditional love and the unconditional love of the universe. After all, it wouldn't be unconditional if I stopped loving them simply because they were acting out of their wounding. While I love them unconditionally, it feels like they are asking me to let them go. So I send them on their way with my love. Whatever is for their highest good is my prayer. May the pain and heartbreak I experienced at their hands turn into wisdom and love. May I find the strength to live fully, love fully, and fully open my heart to life.

Straight Words: *End Divisiveness*

Let your heart love who it loves no matter how much it hurts. Never stop caring and loving who you love. Open your heart now and forever! Let it break you open. Love fully and unabashedly even in the face of divisiveness. Stop tolerating divisive energy from others and yourself. What you really feel is always good. It's good to stop judgments and cruel criticisms against yourself and others. When you take a stand in your heart for what is true, you don't tolerate bullshit from yourself or anyone else. Check everything you say for truth and integrity. Check everything everyone else says as well.

Don't allow divisive people to remain in your life if they are hurting you. You can still love them, just help them back out of your life by speaking the truth to them, setting boundaries, and taking space. Love them from whatever distance your heart deems appropriate. You can always send true love in whatever direction you desire. Don't let anyone take away your ability to love. When you close your heart in pain, you let wounding block your love. Sometimes this needs to happen for a little while or a longer period of time. Always return to the love that is your birthright. Through bathing our wounds in unconditional love, our heart opens just as it needs to.

Game: *Spotting Divisive Energy in Self*

1. Listen to what you are saying to yourself in your head and feel for any self-judgment or criticism.

2. Self-judgment sometimes appears in the form of apologizing for yourself excessively, or being subtly or overtly self-critical. For example, "What's wrong with me for being this way?"

3. When you have thoughts that are divisive, they will feel grating to your heart and sound slightly harsh or feel unloving inside.

4. When you notice any self-divisive energy, feel into the feeling underneath it. Then let go of the energy itself as you breathe out.

5. Breathe in love.

6. Accept the feeling you feel. Stop believing any part of the story the divisive energy was trying to get you to believe.

7. Appreciate yourself for noticing this divisive energy and freeing yourself from it.

Game: *Spotting Divisive Energy in Others*

1. Notice anything the other says that feels judgmental or critical of you or another person.

2. Observe how divisive energy hurts the heart.

3. Notice anytime the other person lacks empathy and says something which feels harsh in any way.

4. Point out what you are noticing and see if the person stops being divisive.

5. Even if you don't do anything about it, noticing and tracking divisive energy is a super power in any interaction. If you can stop divisive energy from taking over interactions, you really have the force of authenticity on your side.

6. If you cannot stop a person from being divisive, you may want to question whether or not you want this person in your life. We want to surround ourselves with the most supportive people possible to nurture our growth.

Final Words: Authenticity and Standing for Truth in a World Full of Lies

When we take a powerful stand for authenticity in our daily life, we change the course of human history. Every act of authenticity is an action toward supporting the heart and all of humanity.

Stand with me as we unite to fight for and make a world that truly works for everyone. Let's make this world a better place one action at a time and one conversation at a time.

What you do matters. Your life is an important part of this web of human life, and is inextricably linked with the web of all life. Let's fight for our hearts. Let's take a stand for the soul of humanity now. This is the only time we have. Let's stand together in love!

Story: *The Hitchhiker's Guide*

In *The Hitchhiker's Guide to the Galaxy*, author Douglas Adams describes a world where the people are ruled by lizards. No one likes the lizards who are ruling, but it's a democracy. In the story, Arthur Dent asks, "Why do they vote for the lizards?" Ford Prefect, the narrator, says something like, "They are afraid the wrong lizard will get in power if they don't vote."

This story is reflective of our culture. In our political system, nearly anyone who wants to be president is automatically disqualified from being a good president. Almost no good-hearted person would want to deal with all the cold-blooded, heartless people in Washington, D.C. or the business world for that matter, as most of the politicians are in the pocket of big business. Human beings are not meant to be cold-blooded. We are mammals and we are meant to be warm. Our hearts are like an inner sun that's meant to care for all things.

Political decadence and evil has penetrated nearly every aspect of our life. It reminds me of the shire in the last chapter of Tolkien's great trilogy, *The Lord of the Rings*. The chapter is called, "The Scouring of the Shire," and is largely omitted from the movies.

Even after the dark lord Sauron has been defeated, the hobbits return home to find how deeply evil has come to their dear and precious shire. The shire represents a land of innocence that is often sheltered from outside influences. There's no innocent land untouched by this kind of evil.

In our culture the evil of disconnection lurks in the shadows everywhere. The economic system rests on the exploitation and oppression of the poor to benefit the rich. It's here in every feature of government, in that government is largely corrupt and serving the interests of big business. It's embedded in the jobs we have if we work at a company that is greedy and doesn't serve the best interests of humanity. It lurks in our family culture when parents judge and discriminate against their children or their children are allowed to engage in cruelty with their siblings or parents. It has crept into many of our romantic relationships and friendships when we engage in unhealthy competition and power struggles.

Anytime we block the flow of authenticity, we block the flow of truth and love. Anytime we judge another, for simply being themselves, we engage in the forces of disconnection that I call evil. Because this disconnection is so deeply embedded in the human being, it permeates nearly every aspect of our culture. And yet, I always believe in the hope for humanity that lives and thrives inside our innocent hearts.

Final Straight Words of the Book:

Being yourself in a world that is often so full of lies is not easy. Authenticity will not always make you popular or help you to be friends with everyone. It will, however, lead to a fulfilling life where you attract the people you are meant to interact with. Living from authenticity and truth is love's favorite place to play. The truth helps us end lies in relationships. When we commit to the truth, we commit to love. As Jesus said, "You will know the truth and the truth shall set you free." The truth is the simple key to freedom.

Unfortunately, our culture proliferates lies. The culture has been propagating these lies for so long that they have become normalized and we take them to be an ordinary part of life. Politicians lie, our economy is based on greed and bad beliefs about money and scarcity, our manners teach us to hide what we really feel, and our relationships often teach us that romance has to be a battle or power struggle.

Until we stop accepting lies in our culture, families, and bedrooms, we will literally be trapped in this hell on earth that human existence has often become. I call it hell on earth because the effects of disconnection make life barely worth living. We are meant to connect with and love one another.

The pathway to liberation is here before you and before us all. When we live in our hearts and serve the truth authentically, we become bringers of light and love. The immense power to be ourselves is our saving grace. Authenticity will lift us from the mire and free us from the illusions of our false world.

I sincerely hope this book helps you embody your own unique authenticity. As much as I'm inspired by the people in my own life such as my father, along with great writers and historians, I've had to find my authenticity on my own. To quote Frank Sinatra, "I did it my way!" Yes, I'm quoting someone else as a way to find inspiration for myself. My way rests upon the backs of giants and all the ones who have shared their wisdom before us. I could not be doing what I'm doing today without all my relations who have carried the torch of humanity and all existence to this point.

You too must do it your own way. No one else can live your life for you. Find the unique expression of your being. When you find it, this kind of authenticity opens a profound doorway to the heart and soul.

As this book winds down, I'd like to share an excerpt from my second book, *Unconditional Eternal Love: A Guide to Love Everyone:*

> Love doesn't need to put on any airs. When we are guided by unconditional love, we are as we are. True acceptance of one's level of self-awareness and maturity is necessary in order to be honest with yourself. Trying to be ahead of yourself, or trying in any way to be different than you are, is the affliction that plagues the human race. These conditioned behaviors have infected humanity and made us almost unrecognizable from who we really are. When we let ourselves be as we are, today, without trying to rush ahead or be more mature than we are, only then can we find true authenticity.

It is my hope that this book inspires your true authenticity. From this day forward, may you live deeply connected with this truth. May your life unfold as smoothly as possible with authenticity guiding the way to your deepest destiny. May the truth of your heart and being be so profoundly irrepressible that authenticity is all you know through all the days of your life. May you walk in beauty with unconditional love within and all around you.

And may authenticity be your guiding star now and forever.

Love *Allways*,

Adam Bulbulia

Made in the USA
Las Vegas, NV
20 September 2023

77865022R00127